LIVING WITH ART

LIVING WITH ART

By

LOUIS CHESKIN

INTRODUCTION

By

ELIZABETH WELLS ROBERTSON

Director of Art, Chicago Public Schools

A · KROCH AND SON · PUBLISHERS
CHICAGO · 1940

To

The Adult Education Movement
with the hope that this book will
help propagate the love for art in
our daily life

INTRODUCTION

IT WAS at my invitation as president of the art department that Louis Cheskin spoke at the convention of the National Education Association in Denver, Colorado, in 1935. I had known Mr. Cheskin both as a teacher and as an artist and I believed that he had a definite contribution to make to art education.

His address exceeded my expectations. Not only did he win the attention of the professional men and women, but he also won the interest of the lay audience who heard the address or who read it in press and magazine articles. This enthusiasm prompted me to urge Mr. Cheskin to elaborate his topic, " Social Forces in Art," into book form. Naturally I am more than pleased to see my suggestion blossom forth into the present volume.

Most books, I find, are a rearrangement of old ideas. A few are original, but many of these are efforts designed to satisfy a small circle of readers. At rare intervals a book appears that projects knowledge of the past and the present into the broad horizons of the future. Such a book is Mr. Cheskin's.

He analyzes a great and vital field and opens new paths into art-consciousness. To him art is neither purely aesthetic nor merely technical. Nor is it to him a human expression the importance of which lies only in the historic or in the merely individualistic aspects. Rather, it is a combination of all of these, each a pillar supporting an edifice housing the aspirations of mankind.

His style is simple and direct, yet he deals with a subject usually obscured in a mass of esoteric verbiage. His book is democratic in spirit and speaks to all of the people. It is not filled with a vague and abstract vocabulary. The correlations and associations of art with everyday problems add immensely to the simplification of his analysis. Mr. Cheskin's audience is not a limited one. He speaks to the layman, yet his message is significant to the modern student and to the progressive educator as well.

ELIZABETH WELLS ROBERTSON

CONTENTS

ACKNOWLEDGMENT

I wish to acknowledge my indebtedness to Elizabeth Wells Robertson, director of art in the Chicago public schools, for her encouragement and advice; to Harry T. Fultz, Illinois director of education for W.P.A., for his assistance; and to the late H. K. Seltzer for his keen interest in my endeavor to find new ways of bringing art into everyday life.

I profited greatly by the suggestions given me by Dr. Clem Thompson, assistant dean of University College, the University of Chicago; Clara MacGowan, associate professor of art of Northwestern University, Evanston, Illinois; and Dr. Reuel Hemdahl, assistant superintendent in charge of education of the Chicago W.P.A. Adult Education Program.

I am grateful to Mr. Henry F. Gilson of the Chicago Board of Education for editing the manuscript.

LOUIS CHESKIN

CHAPTER ONE

WHY THIS BOOK

" *The Entombment* " *by Giotto. Natural form appears for the first time in Christian art.*

" *Baptism of Christ* " *by Perugino, an example of static composition in painting.*

"St. Anne," detail, by Leonardo da Vinci, is typical of the **Renaissance** master's lyricism.

"Sistine Madonna," detail, by Raphael, an outstanding example of **Renaissance** sophistication.

Figure by Michelangelo, an example of the art-ist's dynamic expression.

Figures by El Greco, typical of the Spanish mas-ter's spontaneous, dramatic, flame-like style.

4

" Venus and the Lute Player" by Titian, an example of lyrical composition.

" Venus and Adonis" by Rubens, a fine example of dramatic composition.

5

COURTESY OF THE ART INSTITUTE OF CHICAGO

"Mère Gregoire" by Courbet is a fine example of "organic" realism.

COURTESY OF THE METROPOLITAN MUSEUM OF ART

"Portrait of a Man" by Rembrandt. The ingeniously concentrated light is typical of the Dutch master's style.

6

" Old St. Lazare Station, Paris " by Monet is an impression of light and atmosphere but has little form.

" L'Estaque " by Cézanne, showing the addition of definite form to impressionism.

7

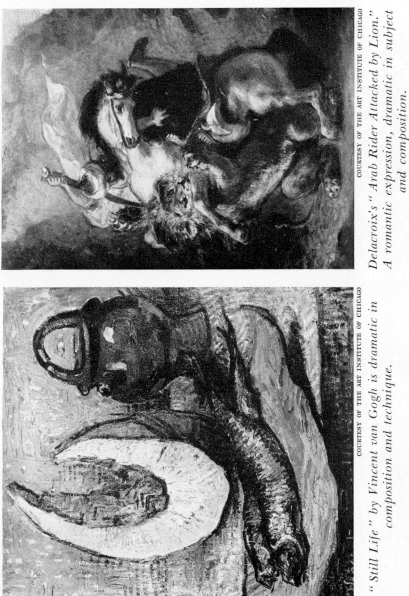

*Delacroix's "Arab Rider Attacked by Lion."
A romantic expression, dramatic in subject
and composition.*

*"Still Life" by Vincent van Gogh is dramatic in
composition and technique.*

8

"After the Tornado," a water color by Winslow Homer, is an example of the American master's spontaneous and dramatic style.

"Romance" by Thomas Benton, an example of contemporary social realism.

Early locomotive designed by an engineer who was not aware that efficiency is related to beauty.

This Santa Fe stainless steel 1800 H.P. Diesel electric locomotive has efficiency and beauty inherent in the functional design.

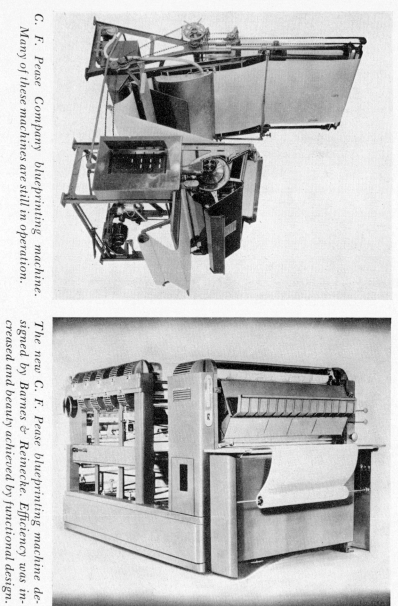

C. F. Pease Company blueprinting machine. Many of these machines are still in operation.

The new C. F. Pease blueprinting machine designed by Barnes & Reinecke. Efficiency was increased and beauty achieved by functional design.

This thermostat manufactured of stamped metal has poor location of controls, dust-catching slots and un-unified appearance.

Thermostat designed by Barnes & Reinecke. Performance was improved and beauty of form achieved.

The first midget radio housed in a one-piece plastic cabinet. The finish is an imitation of marble, the knobs give the impression of carved wood.

Kadette designed by Barnes & Reinecke; smooth surface is characteristic of plastic material. The design is compact, sturdy and beautiful.

Door in the Louvre Museum, Paris, obviously designed to be admired.

Door designed by Abel Faidy. Passive in character, it performs the mere function of a door.

Period interior, an example of a craft concept. It expresses traditional good taste.

Modern interior designed by Abel Faidy, an example of passive design. Simplicity is its keynote.

Crowded interior expressing traditional culture, characterized by an abundance of expensive intricate carving and elaborate design.

Interior designed by Gilbert Rohde. Comfort, beauty and economy are its attributes.

Original Louis XV chaise longue expresses the height of Bourbon luxury.

Corner couch of four separate pieces is the extreme in simplicity. Beauty, comfort and cleanliness are its attributes.

American residence designed in the French traditional style. Ralph Stoetzel, architect

Home designed by Frank Lloyd Wright. Materials from the environment were merged with products of modern industry.

WHY THIS BOOK

A SATISFACTORY definition of art is something I could never find during my entire school life. All the art concepts my teachers put before me were limited in scope, often restricted to a specific geographic area, historic period or social group.

One teacher imbued me with the idea that all classic form is pure art, whether produced by the ancient Greeks or by contemporary painters and sculptors. I learned later that there was no real art until the Renaissance, and also that the era of creative art ended with the Renaissance.

Some teachers assured me that the German artists were unequaled. One kindly old pedagogue saw true expression only in Rembrandt. " Rembrandt injected the psychology of the Dutch people and the character of Holland into his art," he murmured, as if this were a secret.

From a Belgian I learned that there is really only one great artist — Rubens. Later I was made to believe that impressionism is the greatest art. But the worst shock came when I found out that only the primitives and the expressionists produced a vital art, that all other art is cerebral, technical, and, therefore, not art at all.

One professor insisted that only realistic art is great and the rest is merely rubbish. A music teacher held that only music is a true art. Many of my teachers believed that only painting is a true art.

The aesthetes insist that art is purely aesthetic. The classicists declare that art means classicism. The technicians teach that art is technique. The realists cry that art is the representation of reality. The impressionists affirm that art can express only a fleeting moment of reality. The expressionists condemn everything except pure personal expression. The cubists reduce art to a geometric formula. Then there are the futurists, the dadaists, and numerous other cults.

Artists speak about harmony and unity as if these were their undisputed monopolies. Sociologists speak about harmony and unity as if these were significant only to their particular sphere.

The artist has been educated to treat art composition as if it has no relationship to anything else in existence. The scientist concentrates on restricted material aspects of life.

The object of this volume is to bring out and clarify the basic relationship between universal aesthetics, social change, individual expression, and technical accomplishment.

It is my aim to point out that the principles of art composition are identical with the principles of social organization; that the same universal laws dominate the composition of every organized unit, whether that unit is a state or a community, a symphony, a novel, a drama, a painting or a statue.

This book is not intended to be an exhaustive study of art; it aims rather to open up in the reader new channels of thought on the relationship of art to life.

Art has too long been kept in an ivory tower, dressed up in metaphysical, mystical and abstract terms. I have sought to bring it down to a functional level and am therefore presenting my analysis in everyday language.

CHAPTER TWO

UNIVERSAL AESTHETICS AND COMPOSITION

UNIVERSAL AESTHETICS
AND COMPOSITION

ART is primarily an aesthetic expression. Aesthetic expression produces pleasure sensations both in activity and in reception.

The artist derives pleasure from the art of creating or composing because in the process he deals with the basic aesthetic elements: variety, harmony, movement and unity.

The sensation we get from contact with art is that of pleasure. One does not need to be a psychologist to recognize the fact that people would not bother going to theaters, concerts or art galleries if these did not give them pleasure.

Proportional movement in visual art and rhythmic movement in music produce sensations of pleasure. A harmonious combination of two movements increases the pleasure. The complete unity of several combined movements intensifies the pleasure.

The degree or intensity of the pleasure depends very much on the associative process. We enjoy a work of art more if we can associate it with other works of art. Our

23

appreciation is still more enhanced if we can analyze the compositional structure intellectually.

A painting often gives us pleasure through our association of the painted subject with the real. The major pleasure-producing forces, however, are the aesthetic elements; namely, the varied forms and colors in harmonious and unified movements.

Numerous portraits of mothers have been painted, but the painting of " Whistler's Mother " has become internationally famous as a great work of art because the artist expressed the character of his mother not merely in an illustrative manner but in aesthetic form. The elements of serenity, dignity, rest and calm are present in the composition as well as in the subject. The arrangement of the lines, forms and tonal values produces the aesthetic effect. The co-ordination of aesthetic organization with the character of the subject produces the complete pleasure sensation.

AESTHETIC EMOTION

An aesthetic emotion is associated with beauty. It is a direct effect from contact with beauty.

For example, five men look at a mountain. The first man says to himself, " I wonder how much gold there is in them there hills." That is a monetary or economic calculation. The second man says, " I wonder if this mountain was once a volcano. Is this sand rock or some kind of salt or lime? " That is a scientific or geological evaluation. The third man thinks, " I wonder how far it is to the peak." That is a survey of land and an evaluation of distance. The fourth man opines, " I wonder how cold it is up there on the peak." That is a consideration of temperature. The fifth man feels and then exclaims, " How beautiful! How glorious! What a gigantic mass! How purple the shadows are, how golden the sunlit rocks! What forms! How powerful, how rugged! " That is an aesthetic emotion.

We get a greater aesthetic emotion from art than from nature because the work of art is composed, while the part of organic nature that we see is limitless and unorganized. A painting of a landscape is concentrated within a boundary or frame, the colors and forms expressing a complete unit. This is not true in nature.

A work of art leads us through two successive major stages of experience, the aesthetic emotion and the intellectual analysis. The emotion and the analysis depend largely on the observer's education; that is to say, appreciation of a work of art rises from the observer's ability to associate what he sees with what he has previously seen or known.

Only through association is there full appreciation. However, there is no doubt that aesthetic emotion is basically instinctive. Aesthetic emotions are often experienced without any association. Individuals with no knowledge of music have been thrilled by a symphony, and people with no knowledge of art have been emotionally aroused by Rembrandt, Rubens, Leonardo and Raphael.

COMPOSITION

Composition is the art of arranging and of bringing elements into order and unity.

Composition is universal in character and applies to everything consisting of more than one element.

Composition is the art and science of organization. We organize states, cities, clubs, teams, factories, symphonies, and paintings.

It is not the sounds in music that stimulate us aesthetically, but the arrangement of the sounds, that is, the composition. It is not the objects or figures in a painting that stimulate us aesthetically, but the composition of the objects and figures.

A remarkable example of composition and organization is the enterprise of a man whose home was near a row of vacant lots strewn with weeds, rocks and garbage. He organized the boys and girls of the community and set them to beautifying the lots. They collected the garbage and the weeds and turned them into fertilizer; they used the stones to build fences; then they planted flowers which with the help of the fertilizer grew abundantly. What had been a chaotic mass became a composition, a place of order and color; organization grew out of chaos.

The aesthetic principles of organization are the same in the composition of a garden as in the composition of a painting.

Composition and organization are identical. To compose means to organize: organization gives birth to composition.

The tempo of the movement of the lines and forms, the relative intensity of the colors, and the proportion of the values of light and shade decide the character of a pictorial composition.

Variety, harmony, movement, and unity are the basic essentials of composition. Every one of these essentials must be present in some degree in every work of art.

Other aspects of composition are principality and subordination, balance, repetition, contrast, parallelism, consonance, transition, continuity, alternation, gradation, abruptness, and opposition.

The four basic elements — variety, movement, harmony and unity — plus some of the subordinate elements constitute the composition of a work of art.

Art composition is divided into four distinct classes:

1. A dramatic composition contains a maximum of contrast, opposition, transition, and abruptness.

2. A lyrical composition contains a maximum of alternation, consonance, and gradation.

3. A static composition contains a maximum of balance, and parallelism.

4. A passive composition contains a maximum of repetition and continuity.

Extremely active, fluctuating, opposing forms produce a dramatic effect. The forms and lines in a dramatic painting, whether a landscape or a figure, leap and drop abruptly, then rise again. One form rushes at the other, each color is opposed to the one next to it. Sharp lights are set against deep shadows. The opposition, however, is organized, distributed, harmonized. The entire composition is unified into one dynamic movement.

A dramatic composition requires the maximum of control in order to achieve harmony and unity. In creating a dramatic composition the artist must be careful that the major forms do not entirely eliminate the smaller and less important ones. Yet there must be major units that are aggressive and dynamic in their movement, color, and *chiaroscuro* (light and shade).

A lyrical composition is vibrant and delicate. It is never turbulent. It ripples, but never roars. It moves, but never leaps. Its forms and lines have variety, but not too much. The colors are not complementary but are united by a common-denominator color. The lights and shadows merge softly. Alternation of form, soft tonality, and delicacy of color gradation are predominant in a lyrical composition.

A static art composition is not stimulating. It is deficient in movement and lacking in variety because it contains a great number of parallel lines. It is usually symmetrical. Symmetry is static. It produces a perfect effect of rest and is, therefore, an outstanding characteristic of architecture.

When the fourteenth-century artists set in motion the Renaissance by studying ancient Greek and Roman culture, they often employed the classic concept of architectural symmetry in their paintings. Perugino, one of the first masters of the Renaissance, and Raphael, his even more famous pupil, used the symmetrical type of composition in many of their paintings.

The function of a structure is to be at rest; therefore symmetry is a functional quality in a building. A painting should stimulate, should move our emotions and arouse our interest. The static quality of symmetry fails to do so because balance arrests action. It inspires rest and repose.

The passive type of composition is more popularly known as design or decoration. The basic function of design is to soothe our nerves, to quiet our senses. Passive composition is regimented in its movement and lacking in variety.

A curved, soft line is good design but it is not lyrical because it is greatly lacking in variety. The all-over pattern is the most successful design because it is repetitious and continuous, and therefore unarousing but pleasing.

In an all-over pattern, the original basic design unit may be lyrical. The rest of the design units are a repetition of the first, giving the complete design of the cloth or drapery the quality of passivity. The active stimulus is the same as if there were only one small design; the one design unit stimulates, the rest leaves us unaroused, yet pleased by the continuous repetition of the original sensation.

The effect of an all-over pattern is similar to the soothing feeling one gets from resting near a large body of water and listening to the waves. The feeling is psychologically the same. Repetition is the main aspect of the all-over pattern as it is of the movement of the sea.

Passive composition is lacking in variety and its movement is regimented. Static composition is extremely deficient in movement and also lacking in variety. Passive and static art, therefore, are aesthetically of an unaggressive nature; that is, they do not arouse or stimulate, but they are pleasing to the eye. Static form is essentially unobtrusive. Passive design has a soothing quality.

Lyrical and dramatic composition are rich in variety

and movement. They are, therefore, active or dynamic in nature. Lyrical art composition is stimulating. Dramatic art is highly arousing.

SIMILARITY BETWEEN ART COMPOSITION
AND COMPOSITION IN LIFE

Every composition must have variety, movement, harmony and unity.

Society begins with two or more people. An art composition begins with two or more forms or units.

In a well-organized and functioning society there must be harmony in the relationship between the various individuals. A progressive society is active and dynamic. The individuals of a society must have freedom of action and movement proportionally related to the community or state. A society must have unity of purpose and organization.

In graphic and plastic works of art there must be a variety of forms, and there must be harmony between the forms. The forms must have movement and must be proportionally related to the entire composition. A work of art must have unity of purpose and organization.

Because society involves economic wealth, which is the basic aspect of power, man through long periods of history has been denied adequate social organization based on compositional principles. However, in spite of political autocracy or social anarchy, the principles of composition have often appeared in literature, music, painting, sculpture, and in numerous other mediums, because art was dissociated from life.

Pseudo-classicism is generally fine in composition, but pseudo-classicism flourished at a time when life was anything but classic. It was artificially stimulated and deliberately separated from life. Variety, movement, harmony and unity were recognized and respected in art but not in social organization.

But it is in the nature of man to strive for the ideal in every aspect of life. One manifestation of that impulse is man's love for beauty in animate and inanimate forms. Another manifestation is humanity's constant striving toward universal social ideals.

We can presume that the reason we want variety, movement, harmony and unity in art is because we crave them in everyday life. It is logical to deduce that the reason we are stimulated by movement, variety, harmony and unity in everyday life is that these elements are inherent in the universe of which we are a part, and that we are spiritually, emotionally and organically sensitized to these universal values.

Harmony and unity are aspirations of society as well as of the artist. Harmony and unity are as basic in the composition of a society as they are in the organization of a work of art. Variety and movement are just as essential to the social structure as to a symphony, a novel, a play or a painting.

Variety is a basic human requirement. We need variety in our food, in our surroundings, and in our actions. Variety is the essence of art as it is the essence of life. Red painted on a mile of canvas will not be art. C sharp struck on the piano fifty times will not produce music.

Harmony is a primary necessity in community living. When harmony is lacking destruction ensues. Harmony is the basic aspect in family life. Harmony is a primary necessity in a work of art. When harmony is lacking in the forms or colors of a work of art, a chaotic condition exists, and the painting becomes offensive or ineffective. Harmony is the relationship of one part to another. Two units that have a common denominator are harmonious.If people are to have harmony they must have a common interest.

When there is variety and harmony there is proportion. Variety without harmony is lacking in proportion. Proportion is a basic everyday problem. We use proportion in our food, clothes and budgets. Proportion is a characteristic of art. Rhythm in music is the proportional arrangement of sounds. Proportion is a term applied to forms in space (painting or sculpture). Rhythm is a term usually applied to forms in time (music) .

Movement or action is a characteristic of all life. Movement is inherent in the living organism. A painting, drama, novel or symphony must express movement. Lines or forms going in various directions in a drawing or painting produce the sensation of movement. A dot is absolutely static and is therefore aesthetically insignificant.

Unity is a basic community requirement. There can be no group accomplishment without unity. The more unified a group, the more successful it is materially as well as spiritually. There is no art without unity. The more unified the work of art, the more successful it is aesthetically.

Unity is the relationship of all the parts to the whole. Unity is the co-ordination of the various parts of a composition or organization.

PRINCIPLES IN ART AND IN DAILY LIFE

It is significant that aesthetic laws are analogous to social principles and that art concepts and practices are similar to those of everyday life.

A major principle of art composition is not to place the main unit or form in the center of the picture. " Don't stand in the middle, go either left or right," is a counsel we often hear in relation to sociological and economic problems.

The art teacher instructs the student not to place two

units of equal importance on opposite sides of the picture. The political leader demands that the individual make up his mind which side he is on, which party he will support.

The artist explains that a fine composition never has all of the interest concentrated in one corner or on one side of the work of art. The writer on etiquette advises the hostess not to give all her attention, or too much of it, to one guest at her reception, but to attempt to give proper consideration to all.

The artist informs us that a stimulating art composition must have a variety of interesting units. Educators advise us to enrich our lives with a variety of experiences, and they urge us to be open-minded and to explore differing points of view.

The art student is told to avoid straight parallel lines because they are unstimulating. The dietician prescribes a varied diet and points out that the human body cannot thrive on one type of food.

Thus, aesthetic, social and material values are based on identical concepts.

ORGANIZATION VERSUS REGIMENTATION

Each member of a state is part of the social organization. Each form in a work of art is part of the art composition. It is a social crime for one individual to destroy the rights of another individual. It is an aesthetic offense for one form or color to destroy the identity of another form or color.

A completely regimented society cannot stimulate art expression. Ancient Athens and Sparta are an outstanding historical example of a free society versus a regimented one. Athens had a well-organized democratic state under the leadership of Pericles, while the Spartan state was regimented. Athens created a remarkable culture. Sparta left no cultural heritage.

A great and progressive society is active, dynamic. The members of a well-organized and culturally stimulating state are never stereotyped. A great work of pictorial art is either lyric or dramatic. The forms and colors of an aesthetically stimulating art composition are never regimented. Regimented activity and stereotyped form do not stimulate emotion.

Regimentation is the opposite extreme of disorder or anarchy. In a static art composition the forms and colors are slightly less regimented than they are in passive design. Static composition has little variety and even less movement. Passive design is essentially repetitious. Static and passive composition please but do not arouse. We would be nervous wrecks if the endless rows of buildings in our cities were designed to be emotionally arousing. Therefore, static form and passive decoration are employed in architectural design.

The primary function of a machine is to reproduce

an original design. The basic function of architecture is to provide shelter. The machine, being a unit for material production, not only can be regimented but must be regimented in order to function. Neither the modern machine nor modern architecture is created for the purpose of stimulating human emotions.

On the material level, a machine society, like any industrial unit, must be regimented to be successful. But if a society is to be socially progressive and stimulating its cultural and spiritual life cannot be regimented. We must remember that man is an emotional as well as a physical being, that he has spiritual as well as material needs.

Among the most devastating errors of our day is the attempt to apply to the spiritual aspects of life the same forms of organization that we apply to the material aspects. We fail to differentiate between emotional and physical character. It is not yet universally recognized that only inefficiency results when machines are expected to function without regimentation, and therein lies great danger. But the danger to humanity becomes even more acute when we attempt to regiment man's spiritual and emotional life.

While industry is most effective under strict and uniform organization, man's spirit and his capacity for emotion deteriorate from constant regimentation. Regimentation never inspires creative activity and regimented art composition is emotionally negative. Static and passive art do not arouse feelings. Only lyrical and dramatic art composition are aesthetically stimulating.

ART AND NATURE

The classic Greek concept is that art and nature are related, that they move on parallel lines, that they are controlled by the same laws. Aristotle believed that art emulates organic nature, but that it should not imitate the external form or detail of the specific subject. It should idealize the subject and express greater significance than the specific objective reality. This concept of art was emphasized more than two thousand years later by the idealists and pseudo-classicists.

Plato discussed cosmic form and inorganic nature in rather mystical and metaphysical terms. He emphasized the subjective and mental world while Aristotle was interested in the organic and specific. Yet both Plato and Aristotle proclaimed the importance of unity.

Plato's world of idea is a world of diversity controlled by unity; unity is a universal value applicable and related to everything. Although Plato's universals are abstract and subjective, they nevertheless establish the basic concept of an orderly existence.

We must keep in mind that in ancient times science was young; little was known of astronomy and laboratory analysis was nonexistent. Yet Pythagoras believed in a world controlled by eternal harmony, and Plato recognized a world of order. Aristotle emphasized the importance of unity in art in spite of his belief that art should express natural, organic form.

The classic Greeks were advanced enough in their philosophic thinking to conceive a world of order but, lacking modern scientific knowledge, they were bound to organic concepts which were expressed in their crafts and art, in their industry, in their aesthetic tastes, and in their religion. The Greek gods had human attributes.

Yet in spite of the fact that they were limited in their scientific knowledge and were bound to organic values, the ancient Greeks had a remarkable understanding of mathematics. They not only recognized the scientific value of mathematics but appreciated the aesthetic aspects of geometric forms. Socrates said that lines, circles and angles are eternally and absolutely beautiful.

The classic concept of a world of order was developed more than two thousand years later into a pantheistic philosophy by Spinoza, who evolved a mathematical system of thought and analyzed the cosmic nature of the universe. It was Spinoza who first explained in clear terms the difference between organic and universal nature.

Art and nature are identical, if by nature is meant the nature of which Spinoza speaks — the nature of the relationship of the planets, the movement of the earth around the sun, universal nature, not organic matter, not landscape. Composition that is based on universal principles is the foundation for art expression. The nature of organic life, the image of man or beast, is in itself not the essence of art.

We recognize that the diversified cosmic movement is controlled by universal laws of harmony and unity. We know that the movements of the varied multitude of planets follow a universal order of harmony and unity. The laws of harmony and unity as well as the laws of motion and gravity are laws of universal nature. Variety, harmony, movement and unity are aspects of universal law.

Beauty is the visual or auditory manifestation of universal law. Beauty expresses variety, movement, harmony and unity visually or auditorily.

Beauty is inherent in all art composition, plastic, graphic or musical. Composition is the essence of art. Beauty embraces proportion but is not affected by the likeness to the model or by the resemblance to any organic characteristic of the subject. Beauty in art is dependent on its own compositional character.

Beauty, because it is an aspect of universal law, is basic in art. Beauty is not related to or bound by organic nature, except that organic nature also is a part of the cosmic whole and is contained within the universe. We must remember, however, that art, being the product of man, is not a manifestation of pure aesthetics, but is qualified by man's understanding of aesthetic values. That understanding is not fixed or constant; it changes and develops, as do all man's value concepts.

When an artist composes he is aiming to create a complete unit, a diminutive copy of the universe.

A painting, a book, or a symphony is a world in itself, for the reason that it is composed according to the basic laws of the universe.

AESTHETICS AND MECHANICS

The original industrial revolution, which reached a high peak in the nineteenth century, brought about quantity production. The machine eliminated craft from the production of essential consumer's goods.

The champions of beauty, such as Ruskin, denounced the intrusion of the mechanical " monster " into nature's beauty. The champions of the industrial revolution willingly sacrificed beauty for the more tangible benefits of mechanical power. The battle between machine and beauty began.

Often there was a compromise. The locomotive was decorated with cast iron roses in an attempt to compensate for the ugliness of the machine. Many of us still live in homes where the radiators, stoves and furnaces are covered with floral designs.

Another industrial revolution is taking place in our

twentieth century. After more than a century of con-
flict, man has finally discovered that the machine and
beauty are first cousins and have many things in common.

The second industrial revolution is combining mechanics with aesthetics. We have learned that the law
of power and the law of beauty are of the same universal
origin, that mechanical function is closely related to
aesthetic function. Modern machinery is being built on
that principle.

The same principle that gives the streamlined car
its speed also produces its beauty. Man's quest for per-
fection led him to the discovery that physical power
and beautiful form — that is, science and art — are
based on the same universal laws.

Streamlining is a mechanical factor in performance,
an aesthetic factor in appearance, and an economic factor in production. Performance, beauty, and economy
are the triplets of streamlining and the aims of the industrial designer.

The fish and the bird are nature's streamlined models. The motion of a fish or a bird is lyrical and beautiful. The fish glides through the water with the greatest
of ease. The bird sails in the air with the smoothest of
movements.

Artists who studied the fish concluded that its form
is most beautiful. Scientists who studied the fish found

that its form is perfectly adapted to resist pressure in a fluid medium.

Industrial designers took the findings of the artist and of the scientist and created a streamlined design for the modern machine by applying to inorganic form and structure the universal laws governing physics and aesthetics.

However, the universal laws cannot be applied to inorganic form or substance by emulating organic form. Mechanical function is unlike organic function. For that reason the functioning mechanism of the modern aircraft is different from that of the bird or fish. The wings of the airplane do not move like the wings of a bird.

On the heels of artist and scientist came the manufacturer, who is constantly in search of economy in production. He observed first that simplified streamlined forms are less expensive to make. Then he learned that they are more efficient in performance. Finally he found, to his surprise, that the public was attracted by their beauty.

The scientist, the artist, and the manufacturer have formed a triumvirate to create a revolution in the manufacture of industrial products.

Traditional concepts often lead us to believe that beauty and mechanics are separate, even opposed, principles. Many of us still classify people as " artistic " and "mechanical" by nature. The person who is trained in science comprehends and admires the speed of the modern streamlined train, the individual who is educated in the arts enjoys its beauty.

Restricted and limited training often prevents one from understanding and appreciating both the beauty and the performance of the modern streamlined form. However, the public is showing a keen interest in, and is beginning to appreciate, the beauty of the smooth line and significant form of modern industrial objects. People will soon learn that the beauty of the article has increased its performance.

DESIGN AND THE AESTHETIC INSTINCT

It is undoubtedly an aesthetic instinct that causes one woman to appreciate the beautiful figure of another or causes people to admire the beauty of animals. Of course, man admires animals for a variety of reasons, but the lyrical form and movement of the deer and of some horses and dogs are undoubtedly an aesthetic stimulus.

We are also pleased by beautifully formed bottles and jars and beautifully designed wrappers. Recent industrial and commercial reports reveal the power of design. Statistics show that the sales of certain articles have quadrupled after these were attractively packaged. Our love for abstract design shows that beauty is not inherently organic; that is, beauty is not a quality that belongs only to man or animal. The fact that we are unconsciously influenced by design demonstrates that the love for beauty is instinctive.

The aesthetic instinct can be developed or inhibited by upbringing and education. There are many people who look at the Venus de Milo and see a statue of a naked woman. The cultured person views that classic masterpiece as a work of art; that is, he looks at the sculptured form aesthetically.

There is a widespread belief that, because education is required to recognize the aesthetic values of art, recognition of aesthetic values is not instinctive. But as a matter of fact the biologic instincts can be inhibited or perverted just as much as the aesthetic instincts. The reason that the former have not been generally inhibited or perverted is due to the fact that our social institutions have always encouraged and guided their development, whereas the aesthetic instincts have been almost completely neglected during long periods of history.

The rise of industrialism not only brought shoddy products but created the slums and fostered their spread. These filthy, degrading areas had no means at all for developing the aesthetic sensibilities. On the contrary, such an environment was tremendously effective in squelching aesthetic feelings altogether. Even food, the essential for the survival of all living organisms, was scarce.

However, no matter how poverty-stricken a community, it did have a church. The church was the major, if not the only, socially constructive force in the community. In spite of tremendous handicaps, it succeeded to a great extent in guiding the people in their community relationships and in their family living. Thus the biologic instincts were regulated and developed as an aspect of the church's moral and ethical heritage, but the ecclesiastical institution alone had neither means nor ability nor power to influence aesthetic development.

An attempt to develop aesthetic sensibilities required a higher standard of living, or rather a human standard of living. A movement to improve the living conditions of the mill workers meant interference with the profit system. Any such interference was quickly eliminated by the operators.

The materialism created by the factories upset the entire cultural tradition. Art lost its natural function even for the wealthy. The rich found no pleasure in the ugly factories and their products. Therefore they began to glorify the past by collecting antiques and admiring anything that symbolized past civilization. While the upper classes were using art as an escape from the materialism created by industry, the mill workers were finding most of their escape from their misery and squalor in the tavern.

The time has now come when industrialists realize that beauty brings profits. Industry has, therefore, become interested in producing beauty as well as quantity. The aesthetic instincts of the masses are thus being awakened. We have recently learned that the desire for beauty in a product is often stronger than the demand for quality in performance, though the latter is the basic reason for the making of the product. As one wit put it, we used to want automobiles for fast transportation; we now want beautiful cars that give us fast transportation.

The profit motive, which originally brought about the production of ugly and cheap products and more than any other force was killing man's aesthetic instincts, is now beginning to develop those instincts. The slums have not yet been cleared but beautiful objects are to be found everywhere. Beauty is being sold in the five-and-ten-cent store as well as in the department store. It is paradoxical and expressive of our contradictory and transitional social order that we find beautifully designed objects in dilapidated, ugly shacks which some people are obliged to call home.

How did industry discover that beauty brings profits? By laboratory research and because of the collapse of our economic system. In order to revive production, industry was forced to find new ways and means of attracting consumers. It found that beauty is the most effective means.

Commerce does not always use the power of aesthetics constructively. When beauty goes into the making of an article, it is always serving a constructive purpose by increasing the function of the article. When beauty is used as a means of selling an article, it is not always being employed constructively. Very often an inferior product is sold in a beautiful wrapper.

Many people still do not attribute great value to design because they are not conscious of the power of aesthetics. They have no art tradition. They have been accustomed to the ugly and cheap products of the early machines. They have been struggling to earn enough to exist. Many adults have been brought up with, and habituated to, the idea that art or design is merely an unnecessary embellishment, a frill or a fad or a luxury for the rich only.

But people are being greatly influenced by aesthetic forces without being conscious of that fact. Industrial mass production is democratizing life by serving millions of people. Industrial design is on the way to making our environment more beautiful. Our aesthetic instincts are being revived. After we have passed the transitional stage, ugliness may be entirely wiped out. The slum clearing projects of the Public Works Administration as well as of private enterprise have already begun to eliminate ugliness from our landscape.

AESTHETICS AND FUNCTION

Aesthetic form increases the function of an object. The primary function of a chair is to be sat in. Anything that increases the ease of sitting in the chair adds to its function. Carved decoration that annoys the sitter decreases the function of the chair. The modern simplified chair is smooth and spacious, and therefore is most functional.

The secondary function of a chair is to be decorative. Decoration, because its function is to make us feel at ease and produce an atmosphere of restfulness, must be basically passive in character.

Modern workaday life is full of turmoil and unpleasant noises. The modern home is for that reason primarily a place for rest and relaxation. We go home to relax. We find most of our entertainment outside the home, in the theater, concert hall or clubroom, unlike the ancients who sought excitement and entertainment in the home.

The radio provides much stimulating entertainment which can be shut off at will. Carved woodwork and realistic flower designs, which cannot be turned on and off, do not produce an atmosphere of rest.

The purpose of pictures is to stimulate. Chairs and

tables, on the other hand, should be as unobtrusive as possible. Furniture should never stimulate. It should be relaxing to the eye. Dramatic works of art have no place at all in the bedroom. A picture has a specific place in a room. It can be admired at will. We cannot very long avoid the chairs and tables in a room.

A chair should not have sharp, protruding edges. Furniture should not create in us a subconscious fear of colliding against treacherous appendages, or of sitting on a thorn of the rose with which the upholstery is decorated. Truly modern furniture is basically static in form and passive in design, occasionally with a lyrical line.

The smoky and sooty atmosphere of the modern city and the fact that the modern housekeeper is an active member of society and does not cherish the idea of house-cleaning add another function to modern furniture. Simple and smooth furniture gathers less dust than ornate wood carving and is easily and quickly cleaned.

Aesthetics are a factor not only of beauty but of other values in our daily life. Modern furniture, minus the elaborate carving, is more comfortable and easier to keep clean, as well as more pleasing to the eye.

The three functional advantages of the modern simplified chair are comfort, unobtrusiveness and cleanliness.

INTRICACY AND BEAUTY

Intricacy in design is still considered by many a standard of beauty and value. In a craft society, intricacy was an important factor. The more intricate the design the more difficult it was to render and the rarer was the man who could execute it. Intricate design was not only an aesthetic value but also a symbol of distinction. Ornate art became an economic value and a sign of social prestige in the highly developed craft society of the Renaissance.

As the craft society progressed, its art became more ornate. Ancient Greek architecture well demonstrates that fact. The original Greek architectural order, the Doric, was basic and simple. Later came the ornate Ionic order which was followed by the elaborate Corinthian style. Roman architecture was profuse in decoration. The most cluttered types of design are found in Renaissance decoration. The baroque furnishings of the decadent Renaissance period are outstanding examples of intricacy and gaudiness.

Elaborate designs are a manifestation of inactivity. They express the tranquillity and delicacy of the life of the gentlefolk of an agrarian and craft society. Fine embroidered linens and brocaded silks were characteristic of distinction and wealth in pre-industrial society. They were the aesthetic symbols of the leisure classes, which were distinct from the simple and crude craft work of the peasant masses.

Intricate design and fine craft work have no relationship to the tempo and character of an industrial society. Our society is characterized by synthetic materials, fast cars, streamlined trains and gigantic factories that produce articles by the million for the benefit of all the people in a democracy.

Intricacy as a symbol of beauty does not fit in an industrial society. Many of us still look upon intricate design as beautiful because we still think with craft minds; that is, our thought processes are based on craft standards. Industrial standards are expressed in speed and simplicity, both of which are inherent in the streamline.

We are coming to the realization that simplicity is our criterion of beauty, not intricacy. Simplicity is the essence of beauty in a complex industrial society. The love for embroidery is an inheritance from our grandmothers. It is a symbol of the past. Taste for intricate pattern betrays insufficient contact with contemporary civilization.

It is natural and psychologically basic for a simple craft society to find pleasure in intricacy. It is just as natural and as psychologically basic for a complex industrial society to find pleasure in simplicity.

WHY ARTISTS DO NOT PRODUCE
PURELY AESTHETIC ART

The creative painter is concerned primarily with aesthetic expression. His expression of universal aesthetics has three limitations: the limitations of his society, of his individuality, and of his medium.

If the artist's expression lacks adequate organization, it is because his society or his individuality — or both — lacks organization. If the artist's expression is static, it is because his society or his individuality — or both — is static or regimented. If the artist's expression lacks color, it is because his society or his individuality — or both — lacks color.

We must recognize that all mediums have limitations. One cannot make a piano sound like a violin. One cannot make oil paint as transparent or as brilliant as water color, nor can one use water colors like oils.

Perfect composition is impossible, purely aesthetic art is nonexistent, since the medium itself limits the aesthetic expression. The artist, being human, is hindered by psychological and sociological factors. He has moods, loves and disappointments. His work is accepted by one group and rejected by another. His art is acclaimed for a time but later may lose popularity. Social forces affect aesthetics as they do morals and ethics.

CHAPTER THREE

SOCIAL FORCES IN ART

SOCIAL FORCES IN ART

ART played an important part in the earliest stage of society. The first form of society was the cave-dwelling family group. Hunting was the primitive cave-dweller's major occupation and art was about his only other one.

We do not know whether the paintings of the paleolithic family society were related to the hunt in a religious, a superstitious or an illustrative way, but we do know from the paintings that still exist that the art was closely related to the hunt and was integrated in the life of the cave-dwellers.

It is agreed by anthropologists that hunting, carving and painting were the occupations of each man, and that the art was of a highly functional nature and an integral part of life.

The cave-dweller carved his weapons for the hunt out of stone. He painted his hunting experiences on the weather-protected walls of the caves and engraved them on the bones of the beasts.

In the cave-dwelling stage of society, the man was the artist because he was the only member of the family who had experience outside the cave. While the man was out hunting, the woman cared for the young.

The art of carving was paleolithic man's means of making his weapons for the hunt. The art of painting or engraving was his means of expressing the experiences of the hunt.

ART OF THE NOMADIC TRIBES

The major social structure following the cave-dwelling family society is the tribe. There was not sufficient game to feed the large tribes. Therefore, man learned to tame animals, and herding became the main occupation. The tribes became nomads who lived in tents because they continually had to move to new grazing land with their flocks.

The pastoral tribes originated rugs and tapestries because rugs and tapestries were made of wool and were easy to transport. The rugs and tapestries are natural products of a sheep-herding, nomadic society.

The tribal society developed symbols which were expressed in the art of weaving. Pastoral art is abstract, not realistic like the cave-dweller's art. When man ceased to struggle with the wild beasts to gain his living, he was no longer interested in them as a subject for art expression. Pastoral society, therefore, developed the abstract symbol which was inspired by the sky and pasture, by the sun and shadow.

Man wanted to express and record ideas as well as forms and objects. He learned to do this with symbolic pictures. Picture writing was used for many centuries before sound writing and the alphabet were invented. Tribal art, like all art, in addition to aesthetic value expressed many other social values in the symbolism of the design.

In the pastoral tribe the woman did much of the art work, if not most of it. Art craft was the expression of the group. Men and women participated in the making of rugs, garments and other necessary articles. The art spirit was expressed in the making of utilitarian objects. The first step toward equality of the sexes was made in the tribal society, when men and women began to share their creative experiences.

It is very significant that the tribal society which first discovered and recognized the abstract concept of art also discovered and recognized the abstract concept of God. It discovered forces which had no organic form. It conceived powers that were not in the shape of beast or man.

The abstract concept expressed itself in religion and in art. When man first conceived inorganic concepts, he laid the foundation for the ethics and aesthetics of civilization. Thus ethics and aesthetics are an outgrowth of the same basic human concept which was originated in the tribal society on the plains of Asia.

ART IN THE CITY-STATE AND THE EMPIRE

Agriculture became the main occupation as man learned to cultivate the soil. With the domestication of plants man could remain in one location and the city-state was born.

The city-state gave birth to the architect, the artist and the soldier. The architect built the home, the artist decorated it, and the soldier protected it. In the city-state art became a profession instead of a family or tribal expression.

Out of the city-state developed the empire, in which art became a means of propaganda. Egyptian art is basically and mostly a language, a picture history glorifying the king and his deeds.

Egypt, on the Nile, expressed her art impulse in stone. Babylonia, on the Euphrates, employed sand bricks as a medium in which to glorify her wars and kings. Each country developed the medium indigenous to its soil.

In the empire, much more than in the city-state, there developed a division of classes: freeman and slave, rich and poor, king, prince, priest, patrician and commoner, merchant and craftsman.

Art took on a political and class significance. It became a symbol of wealth and power. It became the property, as well as the champion of the powerful and remained such until the rise of democratic Greece.

CLASSICISM

The original classic art was produced in ancient Greece. The age of Pericles is the outstanding period of classic Greek art. The ideals of democratic government were conceived and first practiced in ancient Athens. Great philosophies, magnificent art and architecture, and superb dramas were created in Athens during the democratic administration of Pericles.

Greek art expressed the character of the state and the spirit of freedom. The outward form of Greek architecture reveals the internal structure and character of the building. The drapery of Greek sculpture served to express and emphasize the grace and form of the figure. Athenian art, like the Athenian state, was free, genuine and ideal. Athenian artists glorified life and man. They did not portray individuals. They did not cater to rulers. They sought to express "universals," social ideals. Man, not men, inspired Athenian art.

Not all classic art is significant. With the decline of democratic Athens, art again became, as it had been in Egypt and Assyria, the luxury of rulers and a means of glorifying the kings by representing them as deities. Roman culture was built upon the ruins of Greece. Rome resembled the Greek body but not the soul.

The gods of Rome were not idealized men and women, as in Greece, but the rulers and the masters.

Roman sculpture and architecture were often cluttered with inappropriate, unrelated decoration concealing the basic beauty and character of the form and structure.

Roman art was not spontaneous and ideal. It did not express the ideal of the group, the Athenian " universal." It lacked sincerity and truth; it concealed, over-elaborated, falsified, imitated and flattered. It was neither democratic art nor great art.

THE MIDDLE AGES AND THE RENAISSANCE

When the Christian Church came into existence, it condemned art. Art was the symbol of paganism. Art was associated with pagan Roman and Greek culture. It reflected the physical and exalted the body, whereas Christianity was a spiritual movement. Christianity condemned the human and the physical. It was not concerned with the beauty on earth, but with the life hereafter. It sacrificed the human in favor of the divine.

Representation of the human figure in art was prohibited by the church fathers because it was forbidden by the Mosaic Ten Commandments. Since Christianity originated in the East, Christian art took on the Eastern influence and became Byzantine in character.

Many of the church fathers wanted art as a means of spreading Christianity without glorifying the human body. Therefore, early Christian art represents the human figure as flat, emaciated, abstract and symbolic.

After a dozen centuries had passed, the church did not have to struggle for existence and had no more fear of pagan rivalry. It then began to see in the arts a means of glorifying itself, and so it encouraged the revival of classic culture.

The leaders of the Roman Catholic Church, like the heads of the ancient Roman Empire, employed art as a means of expressing the splendor, wealth and glory of their institution.

The great masses reacted against the denial of the real and the organic. They revolted against the all-embracing authority of the church. They became interested in things of the earth and indifferent to the rewards of heaven. Classic art and literature were discovered and with them the Greek ideas of freedom, science and art. The revival of classic culture in the fourteenth century, which is known as the Renaissance, spread over all of Europe.

Great artists arose who expressed physical values and individual qualities. Man became interested in the physical, in the beautiful and in himself. As in the times of the Greeks, the individual became conscious of his body, of his mind, of his senses, and of his rights as an individual. This spirit also reached the northern countries and there it led to the development not only of art, literature and science but to the Reformation and democracy.

FREDERICK THE GREAT, NAPOLEON
AND PSEUDO-CLASSICISM

The Renaissance became decadent, art insipid, the church bigoted, and free thought and action were suppressed. Monarchy and reaction took the saddle. Art expressed the decadence, weakness and pettiness of the rulers. In France, Boucher and Van Loo expressed the character of the decadent Bourbons.

The Bourbons were overthrown and Napoleon came into power. Pseudo-classic art arose. David became the outstanding painter. The art of Boucher and Van Loo went into decline with the downfall of the Bourbon rulers.

In Germany, Frederick the Great aspired to become as great as Caesar or Pericles. Could there be a surer way to become as Caesar than by surrounding himself with the things that were Caesar's? The dignified and heroic classicism harmonized with Frederick's military achievements. His heroic struggle in the Seven Years' War was personified in the pseudo-classic sculpture and painting.

Frederick the Great and Napoleon glorified pseudo-classicism. These two political giants not only effected political changes but molded the art concepts of their time.

Art, like politics, alters with each social change. Political leaders have recognized art as an important aspect of social organization. Throughout history rulers have used art for their own personal advantage and have employed it as a means of self-glorification.

Napoleon's favorite artist, David, painted the Greek and Roman heroes with much dignity and austerity. Boucher and Van Loo, the favorite artists of Louis XV, produced paintings that are superficial, artificial and licentious, reflecting clearly the life of the court. They look weak and insipid next to the heroic, dignified, austere pseudo-classicism of Napoleon's David.

David reflected Napoleon's character just as Van Loo and Boucher mirrored the Bourbon taste. The two schools of art differed just as much as did the forces which produced them.

THE FALL OF NAPOLEON
AND THE COMING OF ROMANTICISM

The fall of Napoleon marked the coming of romanticism. Romanticism was not only an art movement, but also a social transition. The people tired of emperors. Frederick William, who succeeded Frederick the Great, was not as ambitious or as capable as his predecessor. Napoleon was overthrown and the Bourbons were restored.

The Napoleonic and counter-Napoleonic armies left Europe ravaged and exhausted. The people were pessimistic and forlorn. Chaos reigned. Passionate individualists sprang up, and pessimistic, fantastic leaders arose. The artists of this era, like their fellow men, were erratic, sensuous, dramatic, and often wild and unorganized. The art they produced expressed their temperaments and reflected their society.

In this environment, the people began to despise the classic austerity and dignity. The pseudo-Greek solidity and colorless statuesque painting of the pseudo-classicists, such as David and Ingres, became unpopular. The people began to dislike the long, involved, formal speeches in the plays of Racine and Corneille. They tired of the pure melody of Haydn and Mozart.

They found pleasure in the dramatic, loosely painted, subjective works of Delacroix, in the passionate and colorful plays of Alexander Dumas and the youthful Victor Hugo, in the powerful orchestral compositions of Beethoven and Wagner. The tempo of the age, its struggle, its drama and pessimism were expressed in the arts.

The romantic movement invaded all of Europe in the nineteenth century. In poetry, Coleridge, Byron, Shelley and Keats expressed the romantic spirit in England, Leopardi in Italy, De Musset in France, Heine in Germany, Pushkin and Lermontov in Russia. The dynamic, romantic spirit expressed itself in all the creative art mediums.

REALISM AND THE MACHINE

The industrial machine brought about the rise of the middle classes. The aristocracy looked down upon the mechanical contraptions. The machine became the greatest producer of wealth, and soon its exploiters became powerful elements in society. The role of the traditional, landowning nobility declined.

The coming of large-scale industry caused the decline of romanticism. Mass production brought about a revolution in living conditions. Science and industry created a spirit of realism. When society became realistic in its social and economic life, art became realistic.

The industrial machine was originally conceived as resembling a living organism; that is, it was built in the form of, and made to function like, man or animal. Art also took on a naturalistic, organic form. Art became technical and objective, akin to the machine.

Painting a portrait in a cold, impersonal manner, rendering the subject's features in their true external proportions, is naturalism. Naturalism is one aspect of realism. It is distinctly organic in character. Social realism expresses the social aspect of the subject but not the specific character.

The social realist is not concerned with the characteristic features of an individual but is interested in the subject as a representative of a group, an idea, a region, a class or a profession. The organic realist or naturalist is interested in the specific and detailed characteristics of the subject.

Courbet was an organic realist. Daumier, a contemporary of Courbet, was a social realist. Daumier's paintings and drawings are not objective renderings; they are expressions of group character and social attitudes.

The spirit of realism came first to the countries with the greatest industrial progress. However, it soon penetrated as far east as Russia. In every country writers and painters expressed the realist spirit.

In France, Flaubert and Zola revolutionized literature by writing realistic novels. Courbet and Daumier shocked the French with their realistic paintings. In Russia, Dostoievsky expressed the spirit of realism in his novels.

It is interesting to note that in spite of the fact that Russia was not economically and technically ready for the industrial revolution, it nevertheless captured the spirit of realism and expressed it dynamically in literature. It should be remembered, however, that the Russian writers were in close contact with French art and literature. Many of them lived in Paris.

IMPRESSIONISM AND INDUSTRIAL PROGRESS

Impressionism is realism in a hurry. It expresses the tempo of the industrial era. The rapid expansion of industry made speed a major social characteristic. The new social tempo was reflected in art.

People began to realize that even science changes, that nothing is absolute or static. This realization became the basis for philosophic thought and for art expression.

Spontaneity is a major characteristic of impressionism. Impressionistic painting is based on the philosophy that nothing in life is static. In painting a portrait the artist gets an impression of the person in a certain mood; in painting a landscape he gets an impression of the scene in a certain light. The person changes as his mood changes, the landscape is not the same after the light is altered. Thus everything the artist does is a mere impression.

The impressionists had no interest in organic form but were absorbed in light and atmosphere. New techniques were developed to express light and atmosphere, spontaneity and mood.

The impressionist character showed itself in music and literature as well as in sculpture and painting.

EXPRESSIONISM AND INDIVIDUALISM

Expressionism and impressionism are quite different in character. As the name suggests, the impressionist produces an impression of the subject. The expressionist is not interested in subject matter but is concerned primarily with expressing his own emotions and his personality.

Expressionism in art is related to rugged individualism and laissez faire in business. The expressionist does not create for society any more than the merchant goes into business with the primary motive of giving service to the public.

Just as the basic goal of the merchant is personal profit, so the primary purpose of the expressionist is of a personal character. Both expressionist and merchant consider the public only so far as it helps them achieve their basic ends, which are self-satisfaction and personal accomplishment.

The expressionist is completely subjective; he worships his ego. He respects neither universal law nor his society nor his medium. Above all he is concerned with his own being, with his own individual expression. His concept, interpretation and expression are purely personal and are not intended to serve or to please the general public.

The psychological processes of the business man are usually different from those of the artist. The merchant is objective in his approach to the commercial situation. He evaluates it coldly and impersonally. The artist is subjective. His creation is a direct emotional expression.

Nevertheless, expressionism does have a socially constructive aspect. It manifests a further revolt against organic realism. The impressionists bathed the realistic form in colorful atmosphere; the expressionists eliminated it entirely.

Before and during the Renaissance, zoologic organism and physiological function were considered supreme. A machine could only be conceived as resembling and functioning like a man or an animal. Modern machines are built on the basis of physics, that is, on scientific law. Modern mechanics have no kinship to animal functioning.

The abstract picture, just like the modern machine, is not a reflection or emulation of zoologic character and form. The modern artist is not interested in producing an aesthetic expression by depicting the physical form and action of man or animal.

Leonardo da Vinci, who in his drawings and paintings expressed great interest in organic, realistic form, invented an airplane with wings fashioned like those of a bird. The expressionist or modernist bases his expression on abstract, aesthetic form just as the modern machine designer bases his design on scientific laws.

The abstractions of the expressionists preceded the modern streamlined machine. The automobile no longer resembles the horse-drawn carriage, for the reason that the self-propelled vehicle is now based on laws of design and is completely dissociated from the horse.

Expressionism lost the universal scientific principle

in the chaos of a society full of contradictions. The universal principles of composition can be expressed in machine design because the designer of a machine must limit his subjectivity. The personal style and expression of industrial designing is entirely secondary to the scientific laws of design and composition.

The profit motive has in this case not been a destructive force because, in order to produce a functioning product acceptable to the public, the individual style and expression of the designer have been made to fit into the social plan; that is, a functional, social value was expressed in the product by the designer.

" Fine " artists have not yet been forced into the social scheme. Their product does not depend on the approval of the multitude. There is no profit motive to force the expressionist into seeking wide social approval. His art is a product of distinction rather than of common utility. He does not depend on mass reproduction of his article.

We generally recognize the importance of organization only in relation to the production and protection of material wealth. Thus our factories are superbly organized and our military institutions are completely regimented.

It is amazing that the expressionist should consider his product above social value while the industrial designer should subordinate his expression to social value.

Expressionism has made its contribution. It has demonstrated that art is greater than organic realism, that art is above physical nature. It has shown that there is beauty in abstract line, form and color. Expressionism has failed to demonstrate universal aspects of organization. It is bound to the supremacy of the individual. It has failed to keep up with the industrial tempo, and for that reason industrial art is supreme at the present.

Our entire social structure is not as organized and composed as is the factory. All expressions and creations are not integrated into the social structure. When all human expression is tuned to social needs as industrial design now is fitted to industry and social approval, then composition in art will be given supreme importance.

THE ARTIST AND CHANGING SOCIETY

It has been said that music is abstract and that therefore a great musician is not influenced by social changes. This statement is proved untrue by the music of such a master as Beethoven who greatly changed the character of his music in the latter part of his life. He was influenced by the upsurge of romanticism with its transforming social scene.

We must look at the artist as we do at any other individual. The extent to which a person can change depends on his individual character. Artists like other human beings vary in temperament and personality. Some are easily influenced, others are slaves of habit and do not change easily.

However, social forces usually assert themselves in the younger artists. They are easily influenced by new movements in society, because they have not become habituated to the old forms.

All artists because they are human beings are influenced by their changing environment. The extent of the influence depends on the personality of the artist.

CHAPTER FOUR

INDIVIDUAL EXPRESSION IN ART

INDIVIDUAL EXPRESSION IN ART

PERSONALITY

PERSONALITY is the sum total of an individual's characteristics. Psychologists do not agree completely whether the character of a person is due mainly to heredity or to environment. It is usually accepted, however, that both hereditary and environmental elements form the personality of an individual.

The outward or surface characteristics of a person can undoubtedly be changed by environmental influence, but the basic character is never or rarely changed in the adult. According to Alfred Adler, noted Viennese psychologist, a person acquires the basic characteristics of his personality during the first five or six years of his life.

Personality is a unit; it is a composition consisting of a great variety of elements. Personality like an art composition is complicated or simple, colorful or dull, dramatic or sedate, active or passive.

We often think of personality as a purely individual entity and we are led to believe that individual expression is purely personal. On closer analysis, we find that personality is a factor only in the relationship of the person to the group and individual expression is expression of one person for the consumption or enjoyment of many. We cannot conceive an artist creating for himself and not desiring to show his creations to others. Personality is active only in the group. Individual expression is the medium that binds the individual to the group.

INDIVIDUAL EXPRESSION IN ART

Individual expression in art did not appear to any great extent until the advent of democracy. Individual expression is a democratic concept. The greater the social democracy, the greater the individual expression in art.

In the present day, art in totalitarian countries has no individual expression. The modern regimented state employs art for its own propaganda purposes, as did the ancient empire society. Fascism eliminates the role of the individual as a free agent and therefore cannot have individual expression.

The artist can have free expression only when all the members of the state are free. Free expression in art exists simultaneously with free expression in education and with political freedom.

Individual expression first appears in ancient Greek art. It is very evident in Renaissance art. However, not until the nineteenth century does personal expression become a major social and art factor.

During the romantic era the artist looked upon himself as an inspired spirit and a superhuman creator. The expressionists revived this notion after realism and impressionism had relegated individual expression to a secondary place.

The artist of the Renaissance considered himself a creative craftsman. During the Middle Ages art had no individual expression. The artists were mere craftsmen and technicians carrying out the dictates of the church. Classic Greek art shows individual expression, yet the ancient Greek sculptors were magnificent craftsmen, very conscious of their society and of aesthetic values.

The Renaissance artists did not consider themselves above society. Their art was created for society. They did not think of their personalities as above technical mastery. They had great respect for their medium and mastered it and used it as a means for expressing their compositional and social concepts and individual characters and temperaments. Artists before the nineteenth century considered themselves craftsmen, not ethereal beings.

Up to the period of romanticism, the artist produced his art for a specific purpose. Art had a function; a painting was commissioned for a church, guildhouse or home. The idea of creating art purely as a personal expression was conceived by the romanticists and boasted of by the expressionists.

ROMANTIC CONCEPT OF AN ARTIST

Many of us have been brought up under the illusion that art is something apart from life, that when life becomes boring or weary we run to art for consolation. Art being separate from life means of course that the artist is separated from his fellow man.

The artist has been pictured as a creature of questionable morals who lives in an attic and produces inspired masterpieces to gratify his inborn craving for expression. He exists on inspiration which is supplied by a beautiful and delicate damsel and when the opportunity arrives he partakes of some bread and cheese.

Then one day a wealthy connoisseur discovers his genius and exhibits it to an astonished public. To make the picture even more romantic, the artist's genius is usually discovered when he is on his deathbed, consumed by tuberculosis. This conception of art is held by persons who have not been objective students of art history.

The struggles of the average artist are no different from those of the average young doctor or engineer. The artist who is different is the exception, not the rule. Most of the " different " artists are not great.

Leonardo da Vinci and Michelangelo were not in any way unlike their contemporaries except in genius. Titian was as typical a Venetian citizen as Venice had.

" ARTISTIC TEMPERAMENT "

The " temperament " of artists has numerous sociological and psychological aspects.

Since romanticism it has been traditional for artists to be " temperamental." To the romantic artist, temperament went hand in hand with the black cravat, the beret, starvation for the sake of art and art for art's sake.

Another reason for temperament is that the wealthy sponsors encouraged " artistic temperament " in their favorite artists much in the same way that ancient kings sponsored court fools and royal clowns.

A third reason for the existence of temperament in artists is that many a charlatan can cover up his artistic impotency by being temperamental. Temperament is his individual expression. Many an unproductive and parasitic individual cloaked himself with the mantle of artistic Bohemia not on the basis of endeavor but on the basis of temperament.

" Artistic temperament " is usually mere temper, a cover for sterility, a substitute for productivity and a mantle for egotism. A study of the lives of great artists will show that temperamental outbursts have no relationship to creative genius.

We must consider, however, the psychological aspects of a profession. Not much temperament or richly varied personality can be developed by the process of pressing a lever all day, day after day and year after year. The artist's life is full of colorful experience. He could not create without having that experience. A variety of experiences full of emotional elements no doubt produces an individual of great emotional character.

All human beings are emotional in various degrees. Often the emotions tend to lead to disastrous actions. The brain takes control of the emotions. There is a constant struggle in man between emotion and mind. Mind is the co-ordinator of the conflicting emotions, the force which harmonizes them. The artist is no exception. His mind, trained in the principles of organization, controls and guides the varied emotional outbursts in creative activity.

Some mechanics are more temperamental than some artists. A machinist spends eight hours each day, five days a week, in utterly unstimulating and unemotional activity. But he can certainly make up for the daily monotony by living an extremely varied and emotional life in his leisure time.

Many persons in monotonous and unstimulating professions lead highly emotional lives outside of work hours. Some individuals dealing with stimulating media such as music, painting or sculpture, lead very ordinary lives after work hours.

When man had little or no leisure time he was completely dominated by his profession. With the new leisure, created by an industrial society, man's temperament and character are influenced as greatly by his leisure time activities as by his work.

The true artist is not in any essential manner different from any other professional person. Art is a force for control, not for chaos. Temperamental outbursts show lack of co-ordination and therefore bring out a lack of aesthetic feeling.

The temperamental artists of today are usually expressionists, extreme individualists, who have little respect for aesthetic values, social ideals or technical accomplishments. The socially valuable artist expresses his temperament in his art within the boundaries and control of aesthetic law.

THE IMPORTANCE OF INDIVIDUAL EXPRESSION

Personal expression is of great importance in art. Every artist who has a place in history has expressed in his work elements of his own personality.

The artist's personality or individuality expresses itself in concept, composition, style, technique, color, form and line. The artist puts something of himself into every part of his creation. The simplest composition contains personal elements.

Van Gogh expressed in his paintings his tortured soul, his uncontrolled nerves, his fiery temperament, his hunger for light and color — an uncommon lust for sunlight.

All works of art incorporate individual expression to some degree but often it can only be found by an expert. In great art the personal contribution is outstanding.

Individuality of expression is demanded by the people of every progressive era. Distinctive expression is always interesting. Society will not give an artist great acclaim unless his individual contribution is significant.

Our entire system of business is conducted on the basis of a signature. There is a personal style in the writing of a name, though it may consist of only a few letters. It is easy to comprehend, therefore, how much more opportunity for personal expression there is in the creation of a composition with a multitude of forms, lines and colors.

A pictorial composition is dramatic, lyrical or static, depending on the temperament of the artist and on the character of his society.

A dramatic person like Michelangelo naturally produced highly dramatic compositions, while the cerebral Leonardo created mostly lyrical compositions.

Corot's temperament gave birth to a purely lyrical composition, in spite of the fact that in technique, in atmospheric quality and in color, he was greatly influenced by Constable whose art is highly dramatic in composition.

Titian and Giorgione were alike in nearly every respect. They were trained and later worked together, yet there are essential differences between the two, particularly in the color key.

Monet and Renoir were impressionists. They were contemporaries and interested in the same principles. Each expressed light, color and atmosphere. But there is a great difference between the art of Monet and that of Renoir. Monet's technique is heavy, opaque. Renoir's is transparent, glazed, soft. The physical strength and bulkiness of Monet and the fragile, delicate physique of Renoir are expressed in their techniques.

The romantic Delacroix produced highly dramatic compositions. The dramatic character is expressed in the action of the forms, in the clashing and contrasting colors and in the dramatic subject. Delacroix's technique is labored.

Van Gogh expressed the dramatic spirit even in his technique. The tragedy of Van Gogh's life betrays itself in every brush stroke. A smoked fish, a melon and an apple had no pure abstract and aesthetic significance to Van Gogh as they did to the well-fed Cézanne. To the starving Dutchman the still life was food, a concrete reality. These life-sustaining objects were no mere abstractions. He painted spontaneously with a fiery speed, in fear that his models would spoil and he would lose his dinner. Poverty, nervousness and mental torture are all expressed in Van Gogh's composition, style and technique.

CHAPTER FIVE

TECHNICAL ASPECTS OF ART

TECHNICAL ASPECTS OF ART

TECHNIQUE

Just as the artist must be true to himself, so he must be true to his medium. An artist never uses oil paint like water color, or water color like oil paint, as each of these mediums has its own inherent character.

Misuse of the medium is a falsification and deceit. It also often leads to the impermanency of the work. Water color employed in an opaque manner will crack. Oil used in a diluted form will soon deteriorate. Plaster treated to look like bronze still lacks the durability of metal.

A line medium, such as a pencil, lends itself best to line drawing, while a mass medium, such as sepia, oil or water color, should be used to express mass.

Technique is process, method, skill. Technique is closely associated with personal expression. An artist often changes his technique as he grows older. Titian's brush strokes are looser and more spontaneous in his later works. In Rembrandt's paintings of the later period the high lights are very opaque in an impasto put on with a knife. In his early paintings the high lights are not any more opaque than the shadows.

Corot began in a very hard, finished style. Later his paintings became loose and soft, more in the manner of Constable. Cézanne started by painting like Courbet, then he became an impressionist in the manner of Pissaro, and later evolved his own characteristic technique, a solid type of impressionism.

Technique is always a subconscious manifestation in the master artist, a conscious process to the student.

CRAFT AND ART

There are persons who preach that art is not related to craft because craft deals with mediums which are material and technical. They deny the material in art and disregard the technical phase.

These people are " escapists," running away from the realities of life to the " soothing chambers of art." They foster the conception that art is not material, so that they can escape from actual, real life into an etherial dream world of art.

How can art discard the material aspect when it is created amid a multitude of material problems and things and the medium in which it is expressed is physical? Those who speak of art as being purely spiritual believe of course that people can be purely spiritual. They deny the real and the physical in life as well as in art. The contention that poor craftsmanship produces great spiritual art is like the belief that a sick and weak body produces a great spiritual person.

Drawing, painting and carving are means of expression like speaking and writing. Each art medium has its inherent character which one must learn to understand. Each medium requires the mastery of a technique. The more one is master of his medium, the more fully can he express himself. Only a thorough knowledge of the medium enables a person to express significant compositional form. Great artists were always great or good technicians.

Mere craftsmanship without aesthetic qualities is not art. But there is no art without craft. Craft is the means by which we produce art.

CRAFT AND SOCIETY

Primitive craft is usually very fine art. The primitives created objects that were aesthetically as well as physically functional. To the primitive all utilitarian objects had to be beautiful, and all beautiful objects utilitarian.

The primitives expressed their creative spirit freely, but they did not create decoration which conflicted with utility. Craft was their only means of producing utilitarian objects. The primitive structural design is significant because it is functional, the decorative design is significant because it is subordinated.

The only constructive modern craft is creative craft. The purpose of the modern craftsman is to produce something that is aesthetic, that has individuality, style and expression and is personal in taste and creative in spirit. Modern craft must be creative art. Art is an end in itself because it expresses human feelings and social values.

There are persons who are interested in craft work as a mere escape from idleness. " Solve the unemployment problem by going back to crafts." " Eliminate machinery and return to the good old days of craft guilds." " Bring back the crafts and we'll have no unemployment." These are the slogans of antisocial individuals who are seeking to destroy civilization and to return to the life of the Middle Ages. The shouters of such slogans are either demagogues, willing to sacrifice social progress for the benefit of their personal ambitions, or innocent but blind followers of demagogues.

Craft as a means of producing primarily utilitarian objects has no place in a modern industrial society. The machine is the greatest contributor to the well-being of man. The machine, when properly utilized, supplies the greatest part of our everyday needs and enables us to have a richer and more joyous life, a life spent in creative and stimulated living.

A vase is not less beautiful because it can be used as a container. However, the object of the modern craftsman is to be creative, not to compete with the machine. There is no place for mere craft in modern civilization.

Not long ago I visited a class in handicrafts where a group of women were weaving baskets, evidently for home use. One woman, who was finishing up her basket, said that she had been working on it for six sessions of three hours each. The basket showed no trace of creativeness or design. In fact, it was nearly a duplicate of one that could be purchased for twenty cents.

This was a perfectly healthy woman making a basket. She created twenty cents' worth in eighteen hours. The personal pleasure was of the lowest kind because there was no individual expression involved. The work was mere routine, stifling and positively enervating.

Had this woman need of therapeutic crafts, there would have been justification for this work. But I cannot conceive anything more antisocial than the encouragement of such endeavor for a healthy and normal individual in present-day society.

Significant individual expression is creative expression. Creative expression is vital to every normal individual, if he is to function as a significant, free and contributing unit in a democracy. Art crafts are ideal means with which to express aesthetic and social values.

PERSPECTIVE

Perspective drawing depicts objects as they appear to the eye, not as they actually are.

The reason that objects do not appear as they are is

because the eye is rounded and therefore the brain sees everything through a curved surface.

If you look into a convex mirror you will see changes in all the dimensions of the reflected objects. The convex mirror alters the direction of the lines even more than does the eye.

From infancy we become accustomed to perspective and never think that lines are curved or not parallel to each other because they appear that way to the eye.

To a person standing on a railroad track the rails appear to meet. In reality the rails are parallel to each other; that we know from experience. The rounded lens-like eye causes the two rails to appear as if they meet at a point.

All parallel lines meet at a point on the horizon. In looking at a house on a street the parallel lines of the roof above the eye level appear to come down to a point. The ground line appears to go up to the same point. In looking at a house down in the valley, all the parallel lines go up to a point on the horizon.

There is only one horizon line in a picture. This imaginary line of vision is determined by the eye level. Where this line is to be in a picture is arbitrary.

There is another kind of perspective which deals with mass, not with line. Aerial perspective is the representation of form as it is modified by distance in size, color and tone. As the forms in a landscape recede they become smaller, colder (blue or violet) and fainter in tone.

COLOR

Color harmonies are governed by specific laws. The following principles are functional only in pigments.

Colors are either warm or cold. Cold colors are those which contain blue, warm colors are those which contain yellow. Cold colors recede, warm colors advance.

Blue, red and yellow are the primary colors; that is, they are the colors that cannot be derived by combining two or more other colors. These three colors are called a triad.

A secondary color is one which consists of two primaries. The secondary colors are orange (red and yellow), green (blue and yellow) and violet (blue and red).

Two colors which make a complete triad are complementary. Red is complementary to green because green consists of blue and yellow; that is, red and green are basically red and blue and yellow. Complementary colors are harmonious because they comprise the complete family of basic colors, blue, red and yellow.

Complementary colors intensify each other; that is, red appears more brilliant next to green, orange appears more brilliant next to blue, violet appears more brilliant next to yellow. When complementary colors are mixed they become a neutral color.

Other harmonious colors are those which have a common denominator. Blue and green have a common denominator: blue, because green contains blue. Orange and yellow have a common denominator: yellow, because orange contains yellow.

GRAPHIC AND PLASTIC MEDIUMS

Oil paint is the most common medium and has been the most popular for the past four hundred years. It consists of pigment ground in linseed or poppy oil. Most modern oil paints are chemical products. This medium is popular with artists because it is opaque and lends itself to major corrections. It is permanent, flexible, and rich in color quality.

The second most popular medium today is water color. This medium has been in extensive use for only about one hundred years. It consists of pigment in a glue binding medium dissolved in water. It is transparent and luminous and lends itself to spontaneous expression. When water color is used on a permanent specially prepared rag paper, it is as lasting as oil. However, it lacks the flexibility of oil. It does not permit much changing or overworking and does not lend itself to delicate modeling as does oil. On the other hand, it is much more brilliant.

Water color has been used in an opaque manner and as a transparent wash for many hundreds of years in the East. Only in Europe and America has the medium been looked down upon and did not gain full recognition until this century. The Eastern water color paintings differ greatly in style from the modern European and American water colors. The Chinese renderings are dainty in design, neutral in key and exquisitely delicate in line, in contrast with the spontaneous dashing brilliant water color paintings of the European and American artists.

Tempera is generally used for designs and posters. It contains mostly the same ingredients as water color but is applied in an opaque rather than transparent manner. It is flat in tone and is therefore a favorite medium for design.

Fresco has not been popular for the past three hundred years, but is now being revived. It is a common medium with the Mexican artists, and many Americans are now using it. The process consists of applying pigment to wet plaster.

There are numerous drawing mediums. The common graphite pencil is glossy in quality. The carbon pencil produces a dull effect. There are many kinds of dull and wax color crayons and pastels.

Etching, a process of engraving on a copper plate, and lithography, a process of drawing on a stone, are not as popular now in Europe or America as they were a number of years ago.

In sculpture the Egyptians used stone; the Babylonians used clay; the ancient Greeks and Romans used marble chiefly. Modern sculptors generally use clay for the original and then cast the work in bronze or plaster. Marble, granite and various kinds of stone and even cement are used by many modern sculptors.

CHAPTER SIX

TWELVE MASTERS
FROM FOUR APPROACHES

TWELVE MASTERS
FROM FOUR APPROACHES
AESTHETIC, SOCIAL, INDIVIDUAL, TECHNICAL

GIOTTO

GIOTTO initiated the Renaissance in painting. He was the first painter to react against the Byzantine influence. He discarded the eastern symbolism with its flat, emaciated figures and began to study organic life and paint realistically.

Giotto's art is essentially static. His composition does not give us the feeling of dynamic power or the effect of delicate lyricism. Simplicity is its keynote. The figures are solid and express some feeling of motion. Giotto introduced action in form; Michelangelo later carried it to its extreme.

Socially, Giotto's art is very significant. It marks the break from medievalism. His paintings were among the first expressions of the new thought and symbolized the Renaissance. Giotto was a leader in the movement which recognized the beauty of the human form and the importance of the real and the physical.

We know very little of Giotto's personal life, but we do know that he was occupied very little with piety.

His work shows little mysticism and a great deal of realism, considering the period. The morbidity of early Christian art is entirely absent in Giotto. Individual expression is apparent for the first time since the beginning of Christianity.

Technically, Giotto shows that he was very skillful. Fresco was his favorite medium, oil paint was still unknown. His technique is broad and simple.

LEONARDO DA VINCI

Leonardo da Vinci undoubtedly is one of the most remarkable figures in history. He was outstanding not only in painting but in numerous other fields as well. He was a painter, sculptor, architect, engineer and scientist in physics and biology. He was also a mathematician, astronomer, inventor, geologist, geographer, musician, writer and teacher.

More than any other person Leonardo da Vinci epitomizes the intellectual awakening of the fifteenth and sixteenth centuries. He is the personification of the Renaissance.

It may be that Leonardo was the first industrial designer. He was one master who understood the relationship between art and science. His intensive research in science and in art may have been the initial attempt to evolve the modern streamline design which expresses both physical and aesthetic function.

Leonardo's painting is mostly lyrical, never dynamic. His " Last Supper " is basically static, yet it possesses a great deal of lyricism. Most of the lines in the composition are in perspective, thus relieving the monotony of overparallelism. His lights and shades are subtle, his color is delicate.

He was not a prolific painter, but everything he did was remarkable. He was very much interested in organic form and was intrigued by ancient Greek and Roman art. His portraits have a lyricism, a softness and sweetness which are typically his.

Technically, Leonardo was an experimenter, constantly trying various mediums. His painting was, like his numerous other occupations, a means for research and discovery. He used oil, tempera and fresco.

MICHELANGELO

Michelangelo was a Florentine, but he was also under the influence of Rome. The great activity of Florence and Rome, the power and grandeur of the triumphant Catholic Church, the outburst of invention and discovery, the birth of individualism — all these are expressed and symbolized in his art.

Michelangelo is the most dynamic sculptor and painter the world has ever known. His art is gigantic, imposing and breathtaking. It dominates everything near it.

His composition is the most powerful in history. The human but titanic figures are dynamic, never static; not a muscle is at rest. His compositions do not merely appeal to us, they thunder at us. Static form was unknown to him — even his reclining figures seem as if they are about to stir into motion.

As an individual, he was unique. All his emotion seems to have been poured into his art. The ordinary human passions were not for him.

His emphasis was not so much on the human form as on the pulsating muscles. He was not concerned primarily with painting or carving a portrait. His men and women are universal. His portraits are symbols and personifications, not organic, objective renderings of individuals.

Technically, Michelangelo was a giant. His favorite painting medium was fresco. Primarily a sculptor, his paintings give the impression of painted sculpture.

RAPHAEL

Along with Leonardo and Michelangelo, Raphael is usually considered an outstanding master of the Florentine school.

Raphael's art is generally lyrical. His earlier work is frequently somewhat static. His line is extremely smooth, his form three dimensional and solid, often obviously like that of Michelangelo. In many of his works the form and color are highly reminiscent of Leonardo's. His early compositions resemble Perugino's.

The decadence of the Renaissance begins to show itself in Raphael. Courtesans were the models for his virgins. His portraits are sweet and flattering. He reflects not the power of Florence as Michelangelo did, nor the intellectual accomplishments of the Renaissance as Leonardo did, but the passion and turmoil and the irreligiousness of his society.

Raphael was an outstanding personality, yet his art is not very subjective. He was intelligent and wide awake, handsome, youthful and popular. He was an eclectic and clever student. He wasted no time on experimenting but profited from the experiments of others. Raphael is the least original of the three Florentine masters, yet his art is lyrical, colorful and sweet, and for that reason appealing.

Technically, Raphael was prolific. He died at the age of thirty-seven, yet he produced a multitude of canvases and murals. His technique is not spontaneous, yet not too labored. His drawing is skillful and direct.

TITIAN

Venice was the home of Titian, one of the greatest colorists in the history of art. Just as Michelangelo reflected the grandeur of Florence and Rome, so Titian expressed the splendor and color of Venice, the city of commerce, ships and great homes, the gateway to the Orient of colorful rugs and tapestries.

There are no dynamic, leaping forms and contrasting lights and shadows in Titian's art. It is lyrical, most colorful and subtle. Titian's paintings express sweetness and delicacy. His colors vibrate, they never shriek. His lights are rich and never leap, his shadows are transparent, never empty.

All the sensuousness, paganism and color of Venice are reflected in Titian's art. His paintings reveal little of ecclesiastical influence and none of piety. His works are often religious in subject but hardly so in spirit. Titian is the personification of Venice.

He was not interested in dynamic movements and in symbolic figures. He painted portraits but he excelled in painting the nude. He was an impetuous person, physically powerful and a prolific worker. He died from the plague at the age of ninety-nine, producing great canvases to the very end.

Technically, Titian was unique. He painted not in the common manner and technique, but glazed his colors, putting one thin layer upon another, allowing the lower color to shine through. He thus produced an amazingly scintillating and vibrant effect. With this method he also achieved delicate and soft values. He painted superbly the soft texture and delicate color of the human skin. As Titian grew older his style became more loose and spontaneous.

EL GRECO

El Greco's paintings are full of symbols of the Spanish inquisition. He expressed the passion and the fire of the period, the suffering of the oppressed, the tortures of soul and body, and the turmoil and drama of the inquisition. His elongated, distorted, flamelike figures are dynamic symbols of human struggle.

El Greco began painting in the manner of his master, Titian. He was later influenced by Tintoretto, another Venetian, but Spain, his adopted land, took hold of him and dominated his entire art. The gaiety and subtlety of Venice are not found in his works. El Greco's art reflects the turbulent struggling of a people.

His paintings are dynamic in composition, dramatic in form, color and tone. The forms leap into the air. The masses whirl into one another. The movement flames upward, symbolic of the human soul striving to soar to the heights.

The colors are sharp and high in key in the large masses, that is, in the costumes. The tones leap from deep blue-black to cold white high lights. The background is never flat, it is always part of the tempo of the composition.

The physiognomies are aesthetically negative, but

how the faces intrigue us psychologically! They are cruel and domineering, distorted and suffering, gray and cold, livid, tormented and despotic, violent and tortured, gaunt, grim and severe.

Technically, El Greco was prolific but not meticulous, spontaneous but not finished, skillful but not painstaking.

In composition his art is highly dramatic. Socially it reflects all of the turbulence and cruelty of the inquisition. His style and expression are more subjective than those of any other artist. El Greco is unique in his originality of concept as he is in his compositional force and in his social interpretation and expression.

Considering his work from four approaches, aesthetic, social, individual and technical, El Greco is a unique and gigantic figure in the history of art.

RUBENS

Rubens is the most prolific painter of the north. He is dynamic in the extreme. His art is akin to Michelangelo's and El Greco's. He spent a number of years in Italy, where he studied the works of Titian, Veronese, Tintoretto and the other Italian masters. His compositions are more Italian than Flemish in spirit and manner of organization.

The art of Rubens is powerful in form, strong in color and dynamic in movement. His compositions are never static, his colors always warm, his forms full of force. He was more conscious of composition than any other northern painter.

His great works are Italian in tempo, but his figures have nothing in common either with Michelangelo's sculpturesque, rugged titans or with Titian's transparent and scintillating nudes. Rubens painted the buxom maidens of Flanders. It is in the choice of models that he expresses his Flemish character and taste.

His nude figures are not pretty, nor delicate, nor daintily colored, not pink and sweet like Titian's, nor solid like Michelangelo's. They are real muscle, blood and flesh, naked Flemish women walking out of the bathhouse.

Rubens believed in the life of the senses. He was little moved by the mysticism and symbolism of the church. He did not dwell on any specific or favorite subject. He put cardinals and nudes together as subjects in the same composition. He combined the real with the mythical.

In studying the personality of Rubens we must take into account the fact that he had absorbed the Italian Renaissance at its best. His personality was a combination of Flemish heritage and Italian and Spanish culture. He had the basic traits of a Fleming and the manner and polish of a Spanish grandee.

Technically, Rubens is supreme. He is probably the

most skillful brushman of all the masters. His style is
spontaneous, rigorous and superb. Oil was his favorite
medium.

REMBRANDT

Rembrandt's figures are usually static, often lyrical.
His lights and shadows are extremely dramatic. El Greco
achieves drama by his soaring forms. Rembrandt by his
gleaming lights. Aesthetically, Rembrandt rarely de-
lights with his color and not often does he thrill with
his composition. But never does he fail to move us with
his light and shade. Rembrandt did not depend on de-
lineation to achieve and express movement. His language is *chiaroscuro*. Light and shade are his means of
expressing the character of humanity.

Rembrandt personifies all that is typically Dutch. He
expressed the spirit of Amsterdam and the distinct
qualities of its people as no other Dutchman has done.
He was interested in humanity much more than in composition, unlike the Italians, who were absorbed in the
aesthetic aspect of man rather than in the psychological
and showed greater interest in decoration than in the
subject.

Light is Rembrandt's outstanding individual expression. No master has ever employed lighting as skillfully and as subjectively as did Rembrandt. As Michelangelo is outstanding for his stupendous figures and

Titian for his color so Rembrandt is famous for his light and shade.

Rembrandt did not make a virtue of technique, but he used his medium skillfully. In his late period, his shadows became warmer in tone and his lights were put on with a palette knife in a heavy impasto, making the brilliant high lights permanent.

The Dutch people, a liberal and democracy loving nation, had suffered greatly from Spanish domination. The struggle with Spain had not yet been forgotten. The Dutch loved and still love simplicity and domesticity. Rembrandt's great canvas " The Night Watch " did not express the Dutch spirit. For that reason this painting nearly ruined him. The composition smacked too much of Italian and Spanish influence. In the arrangement of its figures, which gave undemocratic importance to a few of the subjects, it reflected too much the Spanish idea of class distinction.

" The Night Watch " (which is a day scene) is heroic in its composition. It was aesthetically too dramatic and in too high a key for the Hollanders. Rembrandt's art was loved for its expression of tranquillity and human character. Heroic stunts and gigantic compositions like those painted by the Spaniards and Italians were not popular with Dutchmen. Rembrandt's art was known to emphasize the character of the individual, not dynamic forms or dramatic movements.

" The Night Watch " is not a characteristic Rembrandt canvas. From an objective point of view it is a fine painting, but it is not as representative of the master's work as are the single portraits.

COURBET

Courbet's art is aesthetically not impressive. It is solid in form but not dynamic. His color is neutral, clear but not brilliant. His composition is usually well put together, yet rarely does it stir us. It is often static, at times somewhat dramatic.

Socially, Courbet was very significant in his day. His art has none of the exaggerations of the romanticists and none of the dignity and coldness of the neo-classicists. He is a direct and logical product of a realistic society. The industrial growth and Marxian economic theories were his inspiration, as they were the inspiration of his contemporary, Daumier.

Aiming to paint life as it was, Courbet limited his aesthetic expression to the literal portrayal of existing conditions. He was completely absorbed in painting his environment, no matter how revolting it was. He was concerned more with idea than with beauty, more with subject than with composition. He was not interested in the abstract and did not emphasize the aesthetic aspects of art.

Courbet was intrigued by the characteristic, organic

features of his model. He was objective in his analysis, and strictly matter-of-fact in his rendition. His portraits and figures are not symbols of humanity, but likenesses of individuals. His landscapes and seascapes are also literal and objective.

Technically, Courbet was ingenious. He was a master of the oil medium and rendered the three dimensional form with skill.

MONET

Monet is an outstanding figure in art because he introduced a new type of landscape painting. His art is lyrical, not in line but in tone and color. His paintings have a rhythmic movement of light tonalities and vibrations and give us a feeling of air and infinity.

Monet's art expresses first of all the philosophy of change, the idea that nothing is static, that all is in flux. The landscape changes with the sunlight. He therefore based his landscapes on light rather than on form.

His paintings represent the revolt against realistic, organic form and a recognition of the relationship between light and color. His color schemes were based on Newton's discovery of the nature of color and his technique was evolved on the theory that two spots of color next to each other will mix in the eye.

Monet was the first painter to make use of Isaac Newton's discovery that light is color and lack of light means lack of color. For more than a century after Newton artists continued to work on the old principle that light was white. Monet applied Newton's color theory to painting and created a new concept of art, an art of atmosphere rather than of form. Monet was interested in the surface play of light and in color for its own sake.

He applied heavy specks with small brushes. He shows none of the delicacy of his contemporary impressionist, the diminutive Renoir, whose pigments are limpid and transparent.

Monet is important technically because he evolved the technique of painting in broken color. Traditionally, the process of painting was in strokes and masses. Monet began to paint with spots of color in order to produce a vibrant and atmospheric effect. Most of his color values are achieved by putting one spot of color next to the other and letting the two mix in the eye. Thus a red next to a yellow will produce from the distance an effect of orange. This method was developed by Monet to a remarkable degree and became the characteristic technique of thousands of painters, the impressionists.

WINSLOW HOMER

Winslow Homer is no doubt one of America's most dynamic painters. His art is powerful and dramatic. His landscapes are stormy and turbulent, his figures solid and true. His colors are cold in value and neutral in key.

Homer caught the rugged spirit of pioneer America better than any other artist. He shows none of the sentimentalism and mysticism of Inness. His figures as well as his landscapes are regional in character and dramatic in subject and spirit.

He expressed the dynamic character of his harsh environment by painting the whirling wind and surf and the struggle of man against the elements. Winslow Homer's America was still an America of rugged frontiers, of sea and mountain, prairie and forest, not the America of the machine.

The man was as cold as his pictures. He had no love for the niceties of the salon or the theories of Bohemia. He was little influenced by the European schools. He loved the dramatic but was not concerned with the abstract aspects of composition. Though his early works are full of inconsequential detail, in his late period he eliminated irrelevant detail and concentrated on the expression of essential, regional character.

Homer has none of the labored overworked technique in his later period. His style is spontaneous, positive and concise. He was sure of his stroke and confident of his brush. He was a master in oil and in water color.

BENTON

Benton's art is dynamic. His forms are solid and always in action. The colors are powerful, pure and dramatic. Benton uses a great variety of forms in his composition, yet the whole has perfect unity. His art is undoubtedly the most dramatic contemporary aesthetic expression.

Benton represents industrial America as Michelangelo represents the Florentine Renaissance. His aestheticism is not anemic, nor sterile, nor sweetened. It is a dynamic aestheticism, a virile expression of our age. He learned a great deal from the European artists, but his art is American in spirit.

He expresses the tempo and color of the contemporary scene as Homer expressed the ruggedness of his environment. Benton is influenced by the machine as Homer was by the sea.

In individual expression Benton is also outstanding. His forms are distinctly Benton. His colors are uniquely combined and original in character. His compositions have a movement all their own. His style and technique are distinctive.

Technically, Benton uses his medium with great skill. He is master of the small sketch, easel painting and mural. His technique is direct, his forms distinctly rendered. Oil, water color and tempera are his mediums.

CHAPTER SEVEN

WHAT IS
AND WHAT IS NOT ART

WHAT IS
AND WHAT IS NOT ART

ART is aesthetic, social, individual and technical expression.

All aspects of aesthetics are elements of art composition. A harmonious and unified organization of a variety of elements in action or movement produces an aesthetic sensation. Variety, action or movement, harmony and unity are the major aspects of aesthetic expression. They are universal and for that reason are basic in all human expression and appreciation.

A painting, a symphony, a drama are all compositions or organizations containing the basic elements of variety, movement or action, harmony and unity. They therefore produce an aesthetic emotion.

The depth or intensity of the aesthetic emotion depends greatly on the character of the composition, that is, on the ratio or proportion of variety, movement, harmony and unity. It also depends on the associative factor, on the ability of the person to associate the new experience with a previous one. A person will get more enjoyment from hearing a new symphony if he has previously heard symphonies and understands their character and structure. On the other hand, repeated hearing of the same symphony diminishes the importance of the associative factor. Often the surprise of a new and original movement, tempo or arrangement is much more stimulating than the repetition of a previous experience.

Something new about the old is extremely intriguing to us all. We are either indifferent to something completely new or we are shocked by it. We are unmoved when we do not recognize it, that is, when we cannot in any way associate it with a previous experience. We are offended when we find it completely contrary to our experiences or habits.

To some degree the social influence is always present in all art. Even the " escapist " does not completely succeed in escaping his environment. Through the entire history of man social forces have influenced the character of art. Artists are human; they will therefore be influenced by their society.

The social influence is an important factor in art appreciation also. Education and environment determine our associative capacities and therefore control our aesthetic potentialities.

We often fail to appreciate a work of art for the reason that we are either ahead of our time or behind it. Some do not like cubism because they feel that it is an expression of the past, that art is now going into the realm of social expression. Others fail to appreciate modernism merely because they are slaves to their early education and upbringing.

Those who have been educated in Victorian schools can find pleasure only in Victorian or sentimental art, literature, drama, poetry. Those of us who are a little younger and have been brought up under the influence of exponents of " realism " can be satisfied only by naturalistic or realistic art.

We are limited also by our individual characteristics. Psychologists agree that we do not all have like potential powers, mentally or emotionally. We absorb influences and experiences in our own peculiar fashion and degree. Some individuals are strong, some weak, some dynamic, some calm. Expression in art reflects the character of the individual as well as of the society.

Because of our individual characteristics, each of us appreciates art in his or her own limited and characteristic way. Thus some of us prefer lyrical art, while others are moved only by the dramatic.

The medium is an important factor in the creation of art. Each medium has its own technical character. Oil is inherently opaque, water color is transparent. Fresco lends itself to the painting of large solid masses. Oil paint is best for rendering details.

In the enjoyment of art some of us prefer the brilliance of water color, others demand the finished detail of oil paintings; some like a rough texture, others a smooth.

In other arts, the various mediums have similar limitations. The piano cannot produce the tonal quality of a brass instrument; the violin cannot produce the tonal quality of a piano. Some prefer the basically lyric quality of the violin, while others enjoy most the essentially dramatic character of the piano.

DIFFERENCES BETWEEN MUSIC AND PAINTING

The forms we see in nature possess some kind of organization, while the sounds we are accustomed to hear are entirely unorganized. Hence many people associate graphic or plastic aesthetic form with organic nature, but find little relationship between the organized sounds of a musical composition and the chaotic noises of the metropolis.

Primitive man employed his ears as well as his eyes for self-preservation. Civilized people are more familiar with natural forms than with natural sounds, which is another reason why good painting is popularly associated with organic, natural form, while few people expect realism in music. It is a common belief that a painting of a bird should show all the tiny feathers, but few people expect to hear a canary or nightingale in a musical composition.

Organic realism in drawing and painting appeals only to the peoples of the West. In China and India art does not emulate organic nature. Eastern drawing and painting lack depth and solidity. Linear and aerial perspective and three dimensional modeling in graphic art were developed by Western civilization. Sculpture of course is inherently three dimensional but Eastern sculpture is not realistic.

The music of the Orient lacks depth and form as does its graphic art. Eastern music is rich in melody and superb in rhythm, but polyphonic, harmonic elements are entirely lacking and the symphonic form as we know it has not been developed in India and China.

The classic Greeks developed painting into a three dimensional art but their music remained without form and served as a background for the drama. In spite of the fact that the Athenians could not conceive an independent musical form, they recognized the emotional qualities in music and attributed to it great powers.

Music was originally identified with the dance and verse. The dance is probably as old as painting and carving. It plays a major role in the social structure of the most primitive African and South American tribes. Verse is undoubtedly as old as speech. Later, music was used in China, India and ancient Greece in connection with the theater which developed out of the fusion of the dance and verse. Music as an independent art did not come into recognition until early in the eighteenth century.

Palestrina, Bach and Beethoven built musical form as we know it. They developed sound harmony and integrated it with rhythm and melody, the primitive elements of music. With the integration of harmony, rhythm and melody, music became three dimensional and colorful. It assumed its own form and thus became an independent art.

Harmonic qualities were present in Palestrina's composition, but truly polyphonic music was introduced by Bach and developed into gigantic range and form by Beethoven. Other great masters made important contributions to the enrichment of the art of music. Monteverde was a pioneer in modern harmony. Wagner combined music with drama in a manner that differed greatly from the Italian operas. Chopin composed lyrics for the piano. Liszt was a pioneer of the symphonic poem. Tchaikovsky interwove Russian folk melodies into his symphonies.

The invention of modern musical instruments no doubt had a great deal to do with the development of the symphony. It is quite clear that the medium is an important factor in the development of an art. The dance and song are among the first arts because the mediums of their expression, the body and the voice, are parts of man. Painting and sculpture date back to prehistoric times because pigment and plastic material such as clay and stone are parts of man's environment. It is natural for man to express himself through mediums which are either part of him or things around him. As the number of mediums increased with the growth of civilization man's scope of expression widened.

Painting differs from music in

1. Dimension: painting is created in space, music in time.

2. Reception: painting is appreciated by means of the eye, music by the ear.

3. Medium: painting is created in pigment ground in oil, glue or water; music is produced by string, wood or brass instruments.

Man's sensitivity to music does not differ from his sensitivity to painting or sculpture, because the compositional principles are the same in all the arts. We are just as conscious of time as we are of space. We are as sensitive to organized sounds as to organized forms. We are as intrigued by the varied harmonious, unified movements produced by musical instruments as we are by those produced in pigment or plastic mediums.

THREE CLASSES OF ARTISTS

Artists are divided by society into three classes:

1. Those who are recognized by their contemporary society and by the future society.

2. Those who are recognized by their contemporary society but not by the future society.

3. Those who are not recognized by their contemporary society but are recognized by the future society.

The first group of artists consists of those who are original in their art concepts and subjective in their style and expression, yet express a significant aspect of the society in which they live. They lead but they do not break away completely from their contemporaries. They are universal in their aesthetic concepts, but regional and indigenous in their social interpretation. The artists of this first group are nearly always aesthetically universal, socially contemporary, individually subjective and technically masterful.

The second group consists of artists who are usually very conscious of their art. They are often deliberately different in their style. Their concepts and interpretations always fit in with the *status quo*. They usually idealize their environment and flatter their sponsors. They are socially backward and aesthetically pleasing. Their compositions are not original though their personal eccentricities are usually very original. Their subjects are always acceptable, their techniques praiseworthy. They glorify the present with the dignity of the antique. They fear to lead into the future and are, therefore, not recognized by the future.

The third group consists of those artists who express

their contemporary environment in the light of their vision of the future. They are aesthetically universal and socially ahead of the times. They break away completely from their environment and have little in common with their contemporaries.

Van Gogh is an outstanding example of an artist who broke from his environment. While the other artists used static forms, Van Gogh dramatized every brush stroke. While Monet and the other impressionists were objectively depicting atmosphere and getting impressions of forms in sunlight, Van Gogh expressed himself spontaneously in a most fiery and subjective style. While the traditional artists used the brush stroke with which to blend and build form, Van Gogh created drama with each individual brush stroke. Artists before him produced highly dramatic compositions with dramatic forms and subjects; Van Gogh produced movement and drama in paintings of still life. Artists before him painted dramatic, stormy landscapes; Van Gogh painted restful scenes dramatically.

THE SUBJECT IN ART

The subject is important in art for the reason that it provides the basic forms, the tones, colors and movements.

No matter how abstract or purely aesthetic a painter desires his picture to be, he cannot possibly conceive a form that is not found in his environment; neither can the musician conceive a sound that is not found in nature. However, nature's forms and sounds are usually disorganized and therefore have no aesthetic significance.

The choice of subject is generally conditioned by the current public taste. Often an artist deviates from the vogue, and usually pays the price for flouting the public's will by living close to starvation. Socially conscious artists usually choose social subjects. Most artists are not very much concerned about subject matter for its own sake.

From an aesthetic point of view, the subject in itself is of no importance. In composition, the form, tone, color and movement are the aspects considered by the artist. However, to achieve complete unity of expression, we generally do not conceive a lyrical thunderstorm, a static battle or a passive hunt.

Artists do not always achieve complete unity of expression. The current vogue — which is a social force — often prevents the artist from attaining complete unity. For example, the neo-classicist David painted a static battle. The composition consists of dignified, austere and frozen figures. Neo-classicism must stand on its dignity; without dignity there is no neo-classicism.

Fragonard of the Bourbon school painted great trees as if they were delicate little rosebuds. Boucher of the same school painted nude women so sweet and delicate, one would think they were made of porcelain. Human sweetness and delicacy did not appeal to the court of the Bourbons; therefore, Boucher produced porcelain sweetness and delicacy.

The tempo and character of the composition are undoubtedly influenced by the subject. However, the artist's personality often outweighs the influence of the subject.

I have seen a number of artists paint the Colorado mountains. To one artist the mountains were colorful and dynamic. A second artist saw them as colorful but static. A third missed the color and also found them static. One perceived the rugged landscape as a sweet song and it was indeed a sweet something that was painted on his canvas. Another painted the mountains in a misty and mystical spirit. One derived his ideas for patterns and designs from the mountains.

The subject is not nearly so strong a factor in art as is the individuality of the artist. The individuality of the artist is guided by universal laws, influenced by social forces and limited by the medium.

THE ALLEY AS AN ART SUBJECT

The artist deals with human values which are in some respects universal and in a multitude of ways limited locally or nationally. The artist expresses that which affects him. He is affected by the things he knows. If the painter looks out of his window and sees an alley, he will paint the alley. If he sees a boulevard, he will more likely paint a boulevard. The artist generally chooses the subject he knows best.

Aesthetically, the artist deals with forms and colors; the subject is of no aesthetic consequence. When an artist wants or needs a rounded form in a composition in order to create a certain kind of variety or movement, it makes little or no difference whether that form is an orange, an apple or a ball. The color usually decides which rounded subject or object the artist will choose. If he needs a rounded form with a maximum of red and some green in order to harmonize his colors properly, he will of course choose an apple.

The common, dirty alley in the slums has many dilapidated shacks which suggest a multitude of interesting forms, angles, movements and colors. It is not the alley that is important in composition, but the abstract aspects of the alley.

No doubt a harbor and a group of modern buildings with gardens and winding shrubbery suggest numerous forms and angles, movements and colors. Many artists have no opportunity to see these socially more valuable and pleasing aspects of civilization and are conditioned by their everyday surroundings.

Our emotional response to the composition is of

course affected by the unpleasant subject. Consciously or unconsciously we get a social feeling from a condition of chaos within order, of filth within beauty.

The philosophic premise that we appreciate the good in contrast with the bad, the beautiful in contrast with the ugly, becomes a psychological reality when we look at a well-composed picture with an ugly subject.

This unconscious or conscious reaction has tremendous social value and is therefore of great importance. Anything that has social value is significant. The reaction is important because it encourages in people the desire to eliminate the unpleasant subject.

One may ask, If the artist wants people to become disgusted with the filthy alleys and do something to eliminate them why not paint the alley as it is, why compose a picture, why use aesthetic law?

The answer is that if the picture were not composed according to universal law, we would not look at it. We are attracted by the movement of the varied forms, which are harmonized and unified.

We begin to notice the subject after the aesthetic effect has passed. Advertisers know this only too well. The posters they display are so composed in their forms and colors that we cannot avoid looking at them in spite of the fact that we have no interest in the commodity advertised.

A well-composed painting will attract us no matter

how unattractive the subject is. When the artist composes he deals with universal laws, and in the choice of subject he accepts the best material available.

We must recognize that artists do not paint alleys constantly and do not generally or consciously search for the ugly. Social influences usually guide them in their selection of subject matter and the immediate environment makes its contribution to the choice.

SYMBOLISM IN ART

Early Christian art is almost sheer symbolism derived from Byzantine culture. The Eastern schools of art have a great deal of symbolism because Eastern culture is based on it.

The expressionist school of art has a number of symbolists in its ranks. The surrealists are basically symbolists.

None of us is entirely free from symbolism. Psychologically, symbolism functions in the associative process. Symbols, no matter how elemental, often recall and associate vague and distant values, give them form and great emotional significance. One elemental symbol can make us feel and visualize a movement, procession, philosophy, experience, love, passion, hate and disgust.

A symbol can be in the form of a ring, a badge, a circle, a diagram or a color. A composition that is effectively symbolic can be an overwhelming emotional stimulant.

We often mistake symbolic emotions for aesthetic emotions. Two old ladies in an art gallery were admiring a thirteenth-century painting. It was obvious that they were thrilled by the picture. I began a conversation with them and soon learned that they were aroused by the symbolism of the subject and were virtually unmoved by the aesthetic aspects of the picture. The composition and the color produced little effect. The subject of the picture was the crucifixion.

It is, of course, true that we are often moved by aesthetic elements unconsciously. But this painting of the crucifixion was static in composition and faded in color. The facial expression and tortured body of Christ produced an overwhelming emotional effect through its symbolism, entirely independent of aesthetic stimulus.

Another example of the associative process inspired by symbolism is the following incident. A woman and her husband visited my studio in search of a painting for their spacious wall. They greatly admired one of my water colors, painted a number of years before. I was surprised that they should take such interest in the least important of my paintings. My surprise subsided when the lady exclaimed to her admiring spouse: " Doesn't this remind you of the little cottage we had out in the mountains two years ago? "

The association of the picture with a pleasant experience stimulated the appreciation. The aesthetic elements were of very little effect, because the woman could not associate the aesthetic aspects of the composition, which were quite lyrical, with any previous aesthetic experience. She was not trained to recognize aesthetic values. The symbolic emotion overwhelmed any native aesthetic feeling she might have had.

All of us are naturally stimulated by aesthetic organization. Variety, movement, harmony and unity are appealing to every person. However, our libido, our instinct for pleasure, is greatly dependent on habit.

We enjoy an experience more if we can associate it with a former pleasurable experience. Something new about the old is a great psychological factor because it embraces variety and harmony; it adds new interest to an old habit.

We can neither understand nor appreciate anything without the aid of association. If an African native who had never seen a train or an automobile were suddenly dropped into a modern metropolis, he would go mad from fright. Lacking any previous knowledge or experience with which to associate the sight, he would have no comprehension of the function and purpose of the rushing vehicles.

Not only appreciation, but even perception depends on association. Seeing a light in the distance is not perception unless the light can be associated with a house, a beacon, a star or a meteor.

After the associative process has established the perception we can begin to recall more associations in order to reach the stage of appreciation. After associating the distant light with a house we have perception, and after associating the house and the light with a loved one we get the sensation of appreciation and pleasure.

Therefore, in order to reach full appreciation of aesthetic values, we must be able to recognize them. A person who is educated in aesthetic principles and is habituated to recognize them will receive much greater pleasure from contact with them than a person who is unaware of the presence of aesthetic factors.

One who understands the principles of organization and composition and comprehends the universal significance of variety, movement, harmony and unity will have no difficulty in recognizing and appreciating them in art.

The aesthetic elements in art — variety, movement, harmony and unity — are symbolic of cosmic law. Art also contains much symbolism in the color, the form and the subject.

Colors in themselves often symbolize ideas, philosophies or countries. Red has been used as a symbol of revolution, blue as a symbol of reaction.

Forms and figures are often symbols of power, freedom or bondage. The subject is usually symbolic of some social or personal value.

THE FUNCTION OF ART

Art had an important function even in the most primitive society, in the earliest period of man's existence. Man never was a purely biological animal.

Man needs food for his emotions, his spirit and his intellect as much as for his body. Civilization has now advanced to a point where more than seventy-five per cent of man's activities are not biological in character. Man does not spend the greater part of his time hunting for food.

Modern man does not merely crave to sustain life. The chef is more concerned with how the food tastes than with how nourishing it is. Homes are not built merely for the purpose of protecting people from cold and rain. The architect gives great consideration to the design and appearance. A great deal more money is spent for the aesthetic aspects of the home than for mere walls and roof.

A most common misconception of art is the differentiation between the useful and fine arts. The idea that what is fine cannot be useful and what is useful cannot be fine is the invention of a class of people who sought to justify their existence and to glorify their impotency.

The upper classes (so-called) created and developed the concept of " useful " and " fine " in the same manner that they developed the concept of " worker " and " gentleman." A gentleman did not work. A gentleman occupied himself with art. Art as the occupation of a gentleman could, therefore, not be useful.

Fine arts *are* useful arts. When they are not useful they are not fine. One of the major differences between a barn and a house is that the house has pictures and decorations in it. If pictures and decorations play a part in deciding whether a structure is a house or a barn then pictures and decorations are indeed useful. A fine picture is most useful. What is fine is useful, what is useful is fine.

The conception that art has no function means that it has no material, physical function; that is, it does not sustain life in a biological sense. The inference is that because its function is not to sustain life, it is not necessary and therefore not functional. This view puts man in the same category with beasts and classifies him as a purely biological animal.

As civilization advances, man's aesthetic and intellectual needs become greater. Man demands art in his daily living, in his home, in his clothes, in his entertainment. Art *is* therefore functional.

ARCHITECTURE

Architecture is the most basic of arts because it is the foundation of human living. The arts are dependent on architecture. Architecture is the mother of all the arts.

Like every other art, architecture is governed by universal laws of composition, by social values and by the expression of the architect's ingenuity. Like every other art, it is limited by the medium.

The character of architecture changes with every significant change in society — for example, the change from Gothic to Renaissance, from Colonial to American skyscraper — and is enriched by the genius of the creative designer and builder.

The introduction of new materials played an important part in the recent rapid changes in architectural design. The change from stone and brick to steel and concrete caused a definite transition in architectural design. We are now developing synthetic materials which are bringing about another significant change in architectural style.

During the entire history of civilization architecture has been the queen of the arts because it always combined physical with aesthetic function. Architecture protects man from the elements and from his enemies and pleases him with its form, arrangement and decoration.

Modern architecture like all modern art has the quality of simplicity. The architecture of an industrial civilization should express the industrial character inherent in the materials. We should express the qualities of steel and glass as the ancient Greeks expressed the qualities of marble. Simplicity is characteristic of industrial materials and is psychologically appealing to people living in a complex society.

Music and painting are intended to arouse our emotions. We can listen to music or look at pictures only when we are in the mood to be stimulated. But we cannot very well avoid the structures in the street. Architecture must therefore be static, pleasing but not arousing.

The most effective architecture is that which expresses internal function in its external appearance. Fine architecture fulfills a specific purpose and expresses that purpose in its exterior.

Architecture is most significant when it expresses the character of its environment, that is, when it fits into the ground as if it had grown there. A building should be related not only to its immediate surroundings but also to the climate. Ancient Athenian architecture was great because it was indigenous to Greece. It expresses a country of sunlight and of abundant marble.

Ancient Greek architecture is static, as a fine building should be. The purpose of a structure is to be at rest. Athenian architecture is superb in its compositional form. It expresses and tells us about the character of the people that built the structures, the kind of life they led. It makes manifest the greatness of its architects and the beauty and strength of its marble.

Modern architecture should, and no doubt will, express our superindustrial civilization with its steel and synthetic materials. New designs will yet be conceived and new correlations of the physical and the aesthetic will be made. Geniuses will arise who will create new beauty with the new materials and find new functions for them.

DECORATION AND ART

Decoration is abstract; it does not deal with realities. Decoration is never dramatic; at its best it is passive. The most effectively decorated room is the one in which the decorations are least obvious, in which we are at ease but are not conscious of why we are so.

The most decorative dress or suit is the one which does most for the wearer. A hat which attracts attention at the expense of its wearer is not decorative.

Decoration should please, not stimulate. It should put us at ease, not produce emotion. It should make us unconscious of emptiness, yet never make us conscious of form.

The most decorative panel is the one which fills a monotonous space on the wall without making us conscious that there is a panel. A panel to which we are attracted by the subject or composition is not truly decorative but pictorial. A pictorial panel is often art, but not true decoration, in the modern sense.

In the past, two dimensional painting was considered decoration. Art had to be three dimensional. We have recently discovered that the most effective decoration is based on line, space and color without any realistic aspect, even in two dimensions.

In the craft society of several centuries ago, when daily life was quiet and monotonous, people enjoyed intricate decorations and exciting furnishings in the home. In our present industrial society, with its noisy and dramatic life, we come home to relax. We relax best in a passive environment, in surroundings with muted color and furniture that is simple in form and passive in design and only occasionally lyrical in line.

Realistic flowers or animals should not be used in designs for floor or chair coverings. Walking or sitting on realistic representations is extremely distracting and creates restlessness.

An abundance of multi-colored, realistic flower or animal forms on a gown will definitely eliminate the character, form and complexion of the wearer. However, a trinket realistic in form is often an effective accent on a robe, just as a realistic picture is an essential keynote in a room which is completely passive in decoration.

We must keep in mind that simplicity and intricacy

are relative, like light and dark or good and bad. A room or a gown can be too passive. Either can become monotonous and boring instead of restful.

A room with modern, passive decoration and furniture should, therefore, have some positive notes of color and form. Vases and modern statuettes of simple but lyrical form lend themselves superbly to this purpose. The color of the vase or figure to be used depends on the color scheme of the room.

A room with pastel shades of green and brown would be enriched by a few pieces of ceramics or sculpture in concentrated green and brown colors. These should be combined with several two dimensional works of art.

The pictures in a room should always accent the decoration in the same way as the three dimensional pieces. Because of their two dimensional character the pictures should contain concentrated values of both or all the colors of the room; that is, a picture in a brown and green room should contain intense browns and greens.

Whether the color of the paintings should be flat or broken depends a great deal on the light and on the furniture coverings. Individual taste is, of course, an important consideration.

Pictures with broken color (impressionist) contain much light. They have a luminous effect. Pictures with much detail do not fit into a room with passive decoration and modern streamlined furniture because they break the unity of the room. Roughly painted pictures harmonize best with furniture that is upholstered with rough materials.

It is important to remember that the function of pictures and sculpture is to stimulate visually. The function of chairs is to be sat on, not to be looked at. The primary function of walls is to enclose space and give warmth and privacy.

Art is active in character. Decoration should be passive in character. For that reason, chairs should have no intricate carving or all-over patterns of flowers or other realistic forms.

Decoration and art differ in character but they are of equal importance to modern man.

ILLUSTRATION AND ART

Illustration, like journalism, tells a story; a work of art does not merely tell, but makes us feel the story emotionally. The illustration, like the newspaper, should be objective; a work of art is subjective. An illustration is important mainly for the subject it illustrates; a work of art is important primarily for its aesthetic value.

Aesthetic expression is the main objective of the true artist. The social influence, the artist's personality and the character of the medium limit the artist in his aesthetic expression. Because of these social, personal and technical limitations, pure aesthetic expression is impossible and art takes on the semblance of illustration.

The journalist tells us about the villain; he describes merely his external aspects. The creative writer, on the other hand, depicts the psychological elements involved and renders the actual physical actions of the character and makes us feel that he is a villain.

The illustrator makes the subject graphic. The artist expresses the subject with emotional and psychological means. Lines and forms, colors and hues are important in an illustration because they make the subject graphic. In a work of art the lines, forms, colors and hues are in themselves significant because they bring out an emotional response.

ART IN COMMERCE

Unlike industrial art, commercial art does not go into the making of the product. It has no relation to the quality of the article.

Commerce is the dominating force in our society. Art, science and industry have become secondary to commerce. Every day we see newspaper references to the business interests. " We must pacify business." " We should have confidence in business." " Do not interfere with business."

Business is constantly impressed on our minds as the pivot of society. When a man meets an acquaintance in the street he usually asks him not how he feels or whether he is leading a happy life, but " How is business? "

Commercial art is art at the service of commerce. Art in this case is not an aesthetic value but the means used to sell a product or an idea. The product may be good or bad, the idea may be socially valuable or socially destructive.

In commercial art, aesthetic laws, social values, personal expression and technical skill become the servants of commerce, not the collaborators. It is painting used to advertise commodities. The aesthetic elements inherent in art mediums are employed to urge people to acquire an article or an idea.

PHOTOGRAPHY AS AN ART

Photography is a fine art. Photography is also used for portraiture and illustration and for commercial purposes. Millions of people are using the camera to take snapshots of their babies and friends.

Painting is actually employed in the same ways — for portraiture and illustration and for commercial purposes, and also as the hobby of thousands of persons who make pictures with the brush but have no concept of the art of painting.

It can be said that there are more snapshooters than painters and that camera artists are more successful than amateur painters in getting a likeness. It is also true that during the past few years there have been more cameras sold than painting sets.

From the point of view of art camera addicts get no better results than amateur painters. They generally obtain a better likeness than the amateur painters, but likenesses are not art.

The millions of snapshot likenesses lack form, depth and character, and usually have no relationship to the picture as a whole. The snapshots lack variety, movement, harmony and unity. They are aesthetically insignificant and socially meaningless. They express no individual character and the technique consists of pressing a button or trigger; the photo finisher does the rest. The photo finisher's craft is often no improvement on the snapshooter's effort.

Amateur painters are no different. They are also interested in likenesses of their friends and relatives, in copying flowers, apples, pears, grapes and porcelain ducks. They rarely comprehend compositional values. They do not look upon form for the sake of form or upon color for its aesthetic value. The words " variety," " harmony," " movement " and " unity " are still meaningless to thousands of amateur painters, as they are to millions of amateur photographers. The amateurs are entirely concerned with depicting the subject. They are subject-conscious but not art-conscious.

Photography has its masters. Some of our outstanding

photographers are masters of form and composition. Many of them were originally trained as painters or sculptors and later took up the photographic medium.

Aesthetically there is no difference between photography and painting. The difference is purely technical. The painter starts with a blank sheet of paper or canvas on which he organizes his forms. The photographer works on a film emulsion. Both photographer and painter have to compose, eliminate unessential details, subordinate some forms and spaces and harmonize and unify forms, lines and movements.

There are professional photographers who, like some painters, have been guilty of falsifying their medium. Photographers have tried to imitate oil paintings and etchings. Painters have attempted to emulate photography. Both falsifications of the medium are equally unaesthetic. They are the result of a lack of confidence in, and understanding of, the medium and bespeak aesthetic adolescence.

Many photographers recognize the characteristic quality of photography. The camera is becoming a remarkable and socially important medium of expression. Photography plays a part in our society similar to that which drawing and painting played in ancient times. The modern camera has this advantage over painting: it is capable of catching and arresting the most fleeting aspects of life.

John Ruskin believed that one of the outstanding

objectives of art is to arrest and make permanent a significant or beautiful moment. No medium can do that better than the modern camera. With the development of color photography the camera will become more important than ever.

If the camera does not lend itself quite as much as painting to subjective expression, it certainly lends itself better to the expression of our dynamic social scene and the fleeting moment.

FASHION AND GOOD TASTE

Good taste is the result of training and cultivation; it is an aesthetic accomplishment. Fashion has little relationship to art for the reason that fashion is controlled not by creative persons who are interested in raising our aesthetic standard but by commercial interests who seek to create new styles for business reasons.

Service and beauty, comfort and good taste often disappear under the barrage of propaganda and publicity which is dynamically released by the business interests.

I know a well-bred young lady who had been constantly catching colds. She succeeded in convincing her parents that if she had a fur coat she would not catch cold so easily. On a miserably wet and cold day in January I met her on the way home from a shopping tour. She wore her handsome Persian lamb coat and, to my amazement, shoes with open toes. I wondered whether

her pot-shaped straw hat had not caught a bucketful of water — it may be that it was perched on her head for the benefit of the artificial yellow feather that peeped out like an onion sprout.

My friend was no exception. The January street was crowded with well-to-do ladies wearing open-toed shoes and fur coats. Fashion dictated the combination. There is neither taste nor logic in such a combination, but for the present, fashion wins. Good taste and common sense are discarded.

Men also are victims of fashion. Women, however, are much greater slaves to the constantly fluctuating styles. The reasons for that are multitudinous and are interwoven with social, economic, psychological and even biological factors.

In spite of commercial pressure, fashions have improved considerably in recent years. Men are still averse to being freed from the tight collar for fear of losing their dignity and superiority, but women's fashions have been constantly improving in comfort and appearance.

Every progressive movement brings with it a reactionary trend. Pot-shaped chapeaux are a reaction to the progressive movement in the styles of women's clothes. Women's fashions are becoming sensible in spite of the artificially created styles which are forced on the public with every new season.

PRECIOUS METALS AND STONES

In ancient times gold and silver were the only known tarnish-proof metals that could be easily manipulated and fashioned into designed forms. Modern industry can fashion any design from the hardest stainless steel, which is richer in tone and more subtle in brilliance than gold or silver.

Modern alloys are many times stronger and quite as beautiful as rare and precious metals, but we have not yet reached the stage where we can judge things by their present worth. We are still tied to traditional craft concepts, and our aesthetic taste is bound to traditional values.

One of the most common examples of our false standard of values is the esteem in which gold and silver are held in spite of the fact that they are neither physically nor aesthetically as functional as modern alloys. Present-day alloys have permanence, strength, flexibility and beauty.

Diamonds are outstanding for their brilliance and durability. Brilliance is basically not an aesthetic quality but durability makes the diamond important industrially.

The main reason, however, for the great value of diamonds is not their function in industry but their universal use as an embellishment. A greater number of diamonds are fashioned into jewels than are turned into industrial tools.

Many precious jewels are kept safely locked up while their proud owner appears in public with a fine imitation of the genuine stones and no one knows the difference. This shows that the rare jewels are not valued for their beauty but for their costliness and for the prestige they give their owners.

Precious stones and metals are still the symbols of wealth and distinction as they were in the craft society. Their rarity is respected much more than their beauty, as most people cannot tell a true diamond from a manufactured one or a precious metal from an alloy.

RARITY AND THE VALUE OF A WORK OF ART

Art has at the present time a market value as do all other commodities. It is not the aesthetic quality or social usefulness of a work of art that decides its value, but the rarity. Rare antiques are therefore the most costly works of art, regardless of aesthetic merit.

Love for rare antiques is no sign of aesthetic taste. Neither the age nor the pecuniary value of an object makes it aesthetically significant.

However, we must keep in mind that while a rare and old object may not be beautiful to our modern, developed sense, it may still have great value as a rare example of the aesthetic sense of the period which produced it. Objects valuable because of their historic significance belong in museums, where people come to observe or study the history of humanity through its creations.

People often have a sentimental attachment to old objects. The objects may be symbols which call forth the vision of pleasant experiences and thus create pleasant sensations. As such they have human value, but aesthetically they are of no importance.

Taste for period furniture is often a subconscious manifestation of the desire to return to the days of the past. Louis XV furnishings are associated with the Bourbon court. Neo-classic furniture is subconsciously associated with the heroic days of Napoleon. None of the associations are conscious but they are there nevertheless. The fact that we can now possess objects that in former times only kings and emperors could have makes us feel akin to the mighty of the past.

There are a number of psychological factors involved in our taste for antiques, period furniture and intricate patterns. One may desire objects of the past to satisfy his ego. Some use the symbols of a past society as an escape mechanism. They express in their craving for the old a lack of confidence in our contemporary society. There are those who are merely slaves to early upbringing and environment. Then there is of course the idea that " what was good enough for my father and mother is good enough for me."

Many people prefer an original painting by a mediocre artist to a fine reproduction of a work by a great artist for the reason that they prefer that which no one else can have. Aesthetically a fine, accurate reproduction is no less valuable than the original.

The craving for works of art by old masters has no aesthetic significance but is psychologically related to the ego and is sociologically based on economic value. An original work of art gives satisfaction to the owner because, being one of a kind, it has a greater price value than a printed reproduction.

The machine has already devaluated rarity to a great extent because the machine can produce millions of objects as fine as the original. No matter what the political system of a country is, the machine is a regimented democrat — regimented because it is accurately and scientifically co-ordinated, a democrat because it produces millions of identical objects without regard for whom they are made.

We are coming to a point when the rich will have no better products than the masses. The machine is leading toward greater democracy because every year it serves a greater number of people.

We still live under an economy of scarcity in spite of the fact that our machines are producing an abundance of goods and can produce still greater quantities. Our thought processes are still based on the economic hypothesis of scarcity. When our industrial society reaches its peak and craft concepts are entirely eliminated from our daily life, aesthetic values will become more important and rarity and scarcity will be of little significance in our lives.

ATHLETICS AND ART

The function of archery in a primitive society was to provide food for subsistence. The bow and arrow were the primitive's only means of shooting wild animals for food. The primitive exercised his body at the same time that he was getting food. He had very little leisure time to worry about.

In a modern industrial society, we do not exercise our bodies in earning a livelihood. The average modern worker has sufficient leisure but has little or no physical exercise. The present function of archery therefore is to exercise our bodies in a pleasant activity during our leisure time.

The primitives had no problem in securing fresh air and sunshine. The modern dweller in an industrial center must get these essentials for healthful living in sport activities. A function of sports, therefore, is to enable us to secure the necessary fresh air and sunshine.

Sports definitely have an aesthetic aspect. The four major requisites of an aesthetic unit are expressed in sports. Variety, movement, harmony and unity are characteristics of every team. The archer must develop form, lyrical movement and the ability to evaluate proportion in judging distances. Technique is, of course, as necessary in sports as it is in painting or in writing a novel.

In watching a game, or an archer drawing his bow, the observer will get a distinct aesthetic pleasure if he is educated to feel and appreciate the rhythmic movement of the varied forms or muscles involved and the harmonious, unified action. The organization of a ball team is basically no different from any other kind of organization or composition.

Most of us, however, have not yet reached the point of social progress and education where we are able to associate and correlate social organizational aspects, art composition and the organization of games and sports. The classic Athenians recognized the aesthetic aspects in sports as in arts and gave them equal importance in the social structure.

MAJOR AND MINOR ARTS

From a social point of view all the arts are equally important, as all are significant to man's spirit and emotions. It is the cultural limitation of a society that makes one art more important than another.

However, in different periods of history various arts came to the top in popularity. For example, with the reappearance of natural form in the art of the Renaissance masters, painting and sculpture became predominant. With the introduction of counterpoint by Bach and the development of the orchestra by Beethoven, music became very popular.

The talking picture is undoubtedly the most common medium at the present time. The difference between screen and stage is that the stage, because of medium limitation, concentrates on characterization, whereas the screen emphasizes mass movement. The moving picture is often more dynamic but lacks the human contact between actors and audience.

From a psychological point of view drama is the most effective of the arts. Drama stimulates more quickly and more intensely than any other art.

While we receive the sensations from painting through the eye and from music through the ear, drama reaches us through eye and ear at the same time.

While painting is expressed in space and music in time, drama is expressed in time and space.

While painting is expressed in a " foreign " medium about which we may know very little, drama employs the human voice and body which we all know. The medium itself furnishes a common basis for audience and dramatist. The symbols are most concrete and direct. The meaning is clear.

The emotional reaction and the intellectual comprehension are often simultaneous in drama, whereas in music or painting the mental process usually follows the emotional.

Because we appreciate things unknown by associating them with things known, we prefer the vocal concert to the instrumental. We are more familiar with the possibilities and limitations of the human voice. Those not trained to play the violin cannot conceive its full beauty, because they cannot associate the music of the violin with a known experience in the same way they can in the case of the vocalist.

The difference between a musically untrained person's appreciation of the human voice and his appreciation of instrumental music is of course a matter of degree, for we can to some extent appreciate fine music even without knowing the instrument, because of previous experience in listening to music and because we are all naturally stimulated to a considerable degree by aesthetic expression.

We should always differentiate between creative and interpretative art. The major arts, we may say, are the creative arts; the minor, the interpretative. Painting, sculpture, music and literature are creative arts. The vocalist, pianist, dancer and actor are interpretative artists.

CHAPTER EIGHT

THE ISMS IN ART

THE ISMS IN ART

IsMs in art are not characteristic of our time only, as many persons seem to believe. They are basically social in implication and inspiration and are coincident with political movements and sociological changes. Isms in art as in politics are often anti-social; that is, they are of no benefit to the growth and progress of society. The anti-social ism is usually escapist in character. The escapist urge manifested itself in the pseudo-classicism of the eighteenth century and in the romanticism of the nineteenth century. The art produced by the pre-Raphaelites in England is a glaring example of escapism. Also recent expressionism betrays an escapist psychology.

The social chaos of the eighteenth and nineteenth centuries created a desire to escape into a better world. Thus, Kant's idealist philosophy became the basis for German philosophic thought, which spread over all Europe. The idealist philosophy was born out of a pessimistic outlook on life. When idealism is the result of pessimism it includes defeatism and embraces escapism. Kant's premise of a subjective world was a convenient escape from the objective, real but unpleasant world.

It was Schopenhauer, one of Kant's successors in philosophic thought, who conceived the idea that the man of genius is not normal and is not concerned with the specific and immediate elements of his environment. Schopenhauer declared that genius does not need society and is not dependent on that which is outside him, that the consolation which art brings enables him to forget the cares of life.

Kant discovered the world in the mind. Hegel affirmed that all things exist by divine right and disappear by the same right. Schopenhauer believed that life is evil, that pain and suffering are basic, but that the world shapes itself by the way we look at it, that everything exists only in man's consciousness.

Kant's subjectivism not only was the basis for German idealist philosophy, but it provided the seed for the extreme subjectivism of romantic art and literature and it was later revived by the expressionists as a reaction to the realism of the later dynamic industrial development. The German idealist concepts dominated the mind of nineteenth-century man and still linger on in some guise in present-day thinking. Looking at the world through rose colored glasses and employing art as an escape mechanism are practices originally inspired by German idealism.

The great German poet Schiller scorned the life of his period and longed for the days of the Greeks. He was a pseudo-Hellenist. Schiller was not a realistic or dialectic thinker, seeking to make his society better, but he had a sentimental longing for an imaginary state of ideal happiness which he believed existed in ancient Greece. He sought to divert the mind of man from the social revolution of his day to the serene province of art and attempted to teach that the artistic sense, as expressed in pseudo-classic form and style, is most basic in man's progress. He edited a literary journal with that objective.

Goethe looked upon Schiller's undertaking with great favor. Goethe wrote, " There is no better deliverance from the world " of struggle " than through art." He too was a slave of the pseudo-classic dogma. He also longed for Utopia. In his later years he was torn between the ideals of classicism and those of the incoming romanticism. This struggle is expressed in his *Faust*.

There were those who could not remain bound to classic formulas. The social forces were changing and demanded another outlook. So they created romanticism. The romanticists were subjective, erratic and dramatic, recognizing neither ancient nor contemporary principles. They refused to be tied to any formulas or concepts. They defied the ancient Greek as well as the established rules of the academies. Individualism became supreme in the arts and in the mode of daily living.

Many of the idealists, pseudo-Hellenists and romanticists admired Spinoza's philosophy of cosmic law and order. The outstanding thinkers and writers of the late eighteenth and early nineteenth centuries talked much about the universality of Spinoza's philosophy but they did not go any farther and did not find that the universal concepts were in any way related to society. They did not apply the principles of order to life. They did not comprehend universal principles of organization. Philosophy was considered abstract, not functional.

The idealists, pseudo-Hellenists and romanticists did not look upon art as an aspect of life, but considered aesthetic expression above life. They advocated art as a means of escaping from the realities of life. They considered art an opiate, a drug which causes one to forget reality. Thus they successfully discouraged the desire to eliminate the abominable social conditions.

England, the country which took the lead in the industrial revolution, produced pre-Raphaelism, an art of a purely escapist character. The pre-Raphaelites despised industrial progress. They looked upon the machine as a symbol of ugliness and as an enemy of culture. They refused to recognize the changing social order and sought to escape from the industrial environment.

The materialistic and industrial movements had their

beginnings in Italy during the fourteenth century. With the Italian Renaissance in the arts came the recognition of material values and many scientific and mechanical discoveries were made. The pre-Raphaelites considered Raphael the symbol of the material and physical and the antithesis to the spiritual and ideal. They therefore sought to return to the ideals of the period before Raphael, to the era of mysticism, symbolism and spiritualism, that is, mediaevalism.

Realism in art was a natural outgrowth of the industrial revolution. It was a stage of progress which sought to find and express truth and reality. Pseudo-classicism, romanticism and pre-Raphaelism were movements that sought to escape truth and reality.

Pre-Raphaelite art was of the same social character as the earlier back-to-nature movement led by Jean-Jacques Rousseau. Numerous means were created to escape the industrial advance. Many people chose to escape into the realm of art, pre-Raphaelite or pseudo-classic. There were those who craved the imaginative, romanticist painting, music, poetry and drama. Others began to collect all sorts of antiques and relics.

The escapism of the eighteenth century never died. The realist movement caused it to become dormant for a short time, but it was soon revived in the form of expressionism. Modernism, like romanticism and pseudo-classicism, is escapist in character. Expressionists escape into a dream world or to the Orient or the South Sea Isles. Much of expressionist art, like most jazz music, derives its inspiration from Africa.

The genuine and significant contemporary artists and designers have recognized the beauty of the industrial form. The reactionary escapists, often called modernists, prefer the aesthetic concepts of African savages. They have failed to appreciate the smooth streamlined forms of the modern machine and have not recognized the inherent aesthetic possibilities of the recently discovered synthetic materials.

We have not yet triumphed over the birthpangs of industry. Our craft-molded minds cannot digest the dynamic industrial phenomena. We have not yet learned how to meet them. We still fail to realize that organizational concepts must be changed because modern communication tends to draw states and continents into one great commonwealth. We often attribute our present social chaos to the machine. The fact is that this anarchy springs from lack of organization in the use of the machine. We are attempting to fit the machine, which is an organized unit, into an unorganized society. And the academic artist betrays a lack of understanding of organizational or compositional values by producing a well-rendered figure or form that is not related to, or co-ordinated with, the entire art composition.

We still struggle as individuals or at best as nationalities. We act like Robinson Crusoe in a world that demands integration and co-ordination. We fear to meet the new industrial principles because we do not understand them. We are intimidated or led to believe that industrial principles can function within the framework of craft notions. By attempting to reconcile craft ideas with industrial factors we have delayed progress in social organization. Our social anarchy has produced much human misery and has fostered a feeling of defeatism. Therefore, means were found to escape the streamlined era physically, as in our back-to-nature movement, and mentally and spiritually, as in pseudo-primitive art. Our troubled times have made possible the reappearance of escapist art.

Romanticism had its strongest roots in Paris. Some of those roots survived the onslaught of realism and impressionism and sprouted in the form of expressionism. The Bohemia of Paris is directly responsible for most of the bad modernist art. Bohemia was at its height during the romantic era. The romanticists could not solve their economic and social problems. They christened their plight Bohemianism and thus glorified their misery.

BOHEMIANISM

The Bohemianism of artists is not at all what most people take it to be. It is not a voluntary mode of living. It is not and never was an essential for art production. It is a perversion of society and a malady born and first nourished in the Latin Quarter of Paris and thence transplanted to every large city of Europe and America.

Bohemian artists are akin to poverty-stricken professors, unemployed steel mill workers and destitute farmers. The basis for Bohemianism is poverty. All the attributes of destitution are the bedfellows of Bohemianism, which is not any more conducive to great art than to good health.

There is, however, a psychological difference between the destitute laborer and the Bohemian artist. The ego of the average worker is squelched, inactive, unassertive. The artist's ego is always active. Subjectivity in art is the expression of the ego. Art must by its nature assert itself. The expression of the artist's self is an important aspect of all art. The artist cannot admit defeat. He will not recognize obstacles. His self-confidence converts obstacles into attributes and rationalizes poverty into riches.

The medieval masses believed that their faith was prescribed by the Lord; the Bohemian artists have become convinced that their mode of living is part of the creative process. The Bohemians not only accept a situation they believe cannot be eradicated but they glorify their condition. We naturally attempt to glorify or justify that which we cannot eliminate.

Bohemianism went farther: it went into business.

It has been publicized like a fair or circus and sold to the bored, the curious and the gullible. Bohemianism became a commodity with its operators, publicizers, promoters and exploiters. Great profits were derived by all except the Bohemians.

One of the major reasons why much modern art is not social in character is that it has identified itself with Bohemianism. The Bohemian mode of living lacks a socially constructive background and expressionist art is completely lacking in social qualities. Modernistic art flouts its lack of value to society.

Expressionism is the grandchild of a superindividualistic society. Society made Bohemia with its slums and squalor possible. Modernist art was born in the slums of the Latin Quarter of Paris. Society has accepted Bohemia as an amusement center and has recognized expressionism, the offspring of Bohemianism, as a very amusing and worthwhile art.

MARXISM IN ART

The Marxian artist is one who, unlike the Bohemian, refuses to accept poverty as a natural condition. Like most members of revolutionary parties he seeks to better his situation. Few artists arrive at their Marxian beliefs because of social consciousness. They simply conclude that a change in the form of society will improve their economic status.

There are two classes of Marxists among artists: those

who believe that their political opinions have no relationship to their art, and those who are of the con-
viction that their art is a vehicle through which they
should express their political philosophies. Many radical artists are convinced that it is their duty to help
save the world through their art.

Those who hold that their social thinking has ,no
relationship to their art are of course in error. They
cannot possibly create art by playing the dual role of
Dr. Jekyll and Mr. Hyde. Consciously or unconsciously,
the artist's social feelings and beliefs are inevitably expressed in his composition, style and interpretation of
the subject.

Deep social feeling and equally deep art expression
cannot very well be kept apart. If they are separated
it is because either the art or the social philosophy is
not of great consequence to the person.

A study of the works of three Marxist art exhibitions
revealed an utter absence of social values. The paintings
of half-starved people and dilapidated shacks were un-
convincing because they lacked form and were entirely
devoid of compositional qualities.

Gray and brown were the dominating colors. The
pictures lacked variety and were without the semblance
of movement. The sordidness of the paintings was sup-
posed to make one conscious of the disintegration of
society. As a matter of fact the compositionless and

muddy paintings inspired nothing more than the desire to walk out.

So-called proletarian art has never gone very far because not even the proletarians want it. Art must stimulate. There is no stimulation in the depiction of slums without compositional character. We are moved and attracted by forms and colors with universal values — variety, harmony, movement and unity.

Mere renditions of shacks and laborers are not art, for the subject is not the deciding factor. Most so-called proletarian painters are not producing social art just because they attempt to depict their miserable surroundings. Socially constructive qualities in art are inherent in the composition, not in the subject.

It is surprising that those who demand that a completely organized society be created overnight should fail to recognize compositional aspects in art. The lack of organization in the art of some champions of a socialist society betrays a desire for economic redistribution but total indifference to basic social values and truly universal ideals.

The reactionaries who demand organization in art but disdain organization in the social structure are equally guilty with the radical extremists. Both extreme radicals and arch-conservatives betray their real character in their diverse attitudes toward art and society.

The traditionalists demand composition in art but insist on laissez faire in economic production and distribution. The political revolutionaries proclaim as their goal organization of our economy but show no interest in the composition and form of other human activities.

Most Marxist artists fail completely in getting their message across because their works have no aesthetic qualities to attract an audience. Order and beauty of composition are lacking. The unpleasant subject attracts no one and thus affects no one.

Truly social art is based on compositional form. Organization is the essence of art and the basis of society.

THE CÉZANNE CULT

No modernist has received as much acclaim as Cézanne. He is hailed as undisputed monarch of expressionism. One can learn little about his art from the abstract verbiage in which his admirers have expressed their enthusiasm. However, the paintings themselves show certain valuable contributions to art.

Cézanne wanted to make impressionism solid. Monet sacrificed form and solidity for the sake of atmosphere and color. Cézanne sought to retain the atmospheric and color qualities and at the same time create significant form. He appreciated the contribution of the impressionists, but he also admired the form and composition of the old masters.

The old masters built up their compositions in three stages: first the composition was completed as a line drawing, then as a light and shade painting in one color, and finally the rest of the color was applied to the form. The impressionists applied the color directly to the canvas in order to gain luminosity and atmosphere. However, they lost the form in the process.

Cézanne attempted to build form directly with the brush. Since he recognized color as an inherent part of form, he believed that the form should be built with color. Why paint the face white or gray or brown and then superimpose the natural color? Pink skin with reflected color from the costume and background should be painted directly on the canvas with the colors as they are seen.

Cézanne's paintings are vibrant in color and plastic in form. His composition is mediocre. It is usually static and often repetitious. His arrangements of forms are monotonous and his figures are stiff and clumsy. His works show some knowledge of composition but no great feeling for organization.

Cézanne undoubtedly had an important principle. He combined the form of the old masters with the color of the impressionists. He not only created atmosphere and luminosity with pigment but at the same time built solid form. His approach was scientific and his objective was significant.

In his early days Cézanne painted, like Courbet, in the academic manner. After studying the impressionists he acquired a style and technique akin to those of Pissarro. He then proceeded to combine the academic and impressionist principles and produced a solid type of impressionism.

Cézanne succeeded in giving form to impressionism. What is very significant is that more than any other painter he showed that form and color are one. He was the first modernist to look upon his subject as an abstract form, as a purely aesthetic unit.

In spite of his limitations, Cézanne led into the future. He created the kernel of abstract art. He eliminated realistic, organic values from aesthetic form. He recognized form as an aesthetic entity in itself and color as an inherent part of form.

Great numbers of people mistake eccentricities for genius. The modernists emulated all the weaknesses of Cézanne and missed most of his constructive contribution. They glorified his failures and his deficiencies and took little notice of his accomplishments.

The expressionists created a Cézanne cult and wove myths around their hero. They invented a special vocabulary and a mystical language with which to honor the obscure aspects of his work. Cézanne has been imitated by hundreds of artists and perverted by many of them.

Followers of Cézanne have in his name created all sorts of pictorial atrocities. Art is not unlike other human activities. Many atrocities have been committed in the name of love, religion and justice. Why should art be an exception? Aesthetic atrocities are committed for the same variety of reasons as are other anti-social acts.

PSEUDO-PRIMITIVES AND DREAMERS

There is a distinct similarity between many modern art exhibitions, showings of children's work, and collections of Eastern art expressions. Modernist artists and their champions proclaim their kinship to child art, African art and Oriental art. The naive, the childlike and even the savage are held up as remarkable qualities in modernist art.

The first impression we get from an exhibition of modernist art is that it betrays a lack of skill, that the painters have failed to master their medium and their materials. Some painters show that they have not even learned to see proportion correctly, to mix colors harmoniously or to apply the paint skillfully.

On further analysis, we find modernist art betraying much more than mere lack of technical dexterity. It reveals as well the psychological make-up of the artist and the character of the social conditions in which he works. Fear, insecurity, indifference to social values manifest themselves glaringly.

Why do artists escape to the Orient, to primitive islands, to ancient Greece and to the dream world? Why revert to the child stage? The reasons are multitudinous but basically social. The answer is simple and direct: fear, insecurity, lack of a feeling of community with our fellow humans bring about a desire to escape from reality.

Henri Rousseau is called a primitive by the modernist champions. He was a petty French customshouse official who began to paint after the age of forty. His creations are childlike, naive. Yet these infantile efforts are hailed by many as pure expression, as art that has the purity of the genuinely primitive. His works are hung in our best galleries and large sums of money are paid for them.

Rousseau's paintings are among the most infantile of the modernistic jumbles. Were his paintings the works of a child they might be viewed as such. To say the least, Rousseau's paintings show not the slightest knowledge of his medium or understanding or feeling for color. They express nothing that is organized, mature, cultured, fine or stimulating.

Gauguin left Paris and went to Tahiti in order to be free to produce pure, primitive art. He wanted to rid himself of the responsibilities of civilization. He sought to enter into primitive nature. He discarded what he considered the empty cares of modern society, yet he had no desire to forget his French audience. Unlike the primitives, he produced art not as an aesthetic, religious or superstitious expression but as a commodity, as merchandise to be sold on the French market.

Gauguin's art is, of course, not truly primitive. His European background could not be discarded by mere fancy or will. His subjects are Tahitian but his expression is not. Gauguin could not possibly become a genuine primitive. He was as much a misfit in Tahiti as he was in Paris. He was mostly conscious of his libido and his ego and sought to satisfy his sensuousness and his selfishness. He had no social ties and his art has no social significance.

Matisse remains in his Paris studio which is his haven and escape from life. He has none of the barbaric mannerisms of Gauguin. He is a typical French bourgeois in every aspect of his daily life except his art. His paintings are artificial, gaudy, formless and incomprehensible. They have no meaning to anyone except to the individual who is willing to study the personal language of Matisse. His art is distinct in style but has no communicative quality, nor is it very functional as decoration.

The design in his paintings is often charming but

childlike. Most of his patterns are borrowed from Eastern art. In his sculpture Matisse goes back to the primitive Africans for his inspiration. His studio is a refuge from modern civilization and his art reflects the character of the refuge but has no kinship to modern Parisian life. His expression is strictly personal, without human ties or social values.

Picasso expresses still another type of superindividualism. He does not concentrate on a unique pattern or original color scheme like Matisse. He is an innovator at best. His art is characterized by periods, each representing another style, another trick and a new idea. His art expression is a conglomeration of formulas that are strictly personal and are not intended to be enjoyed or understood.

In composition Picasso's art is negative. It is static at best. His primitive-looking as well as his classic-appearing slender figures are solid but motionless. His abstracts are usually unorganized, though occasionally they are fair patterns. His line drawings are at times lyrical and interesting and his paintings show skill in technique but they have no relation to modern ideals. They shock and bewilder; they break with the art concepts of the past and they fail to lead into the future.

Surrealism is the most obvious absurdity of all the modernistic stunts. Surrealism, meaning realism that goes beyond the realistic, not only is expression without organization, but it deliberately neglects composition and prides itself on its incongruity. The surrealists do things in reverse and paint things upside down.

The titles the surrealists give their works are usually as incongruous as the works themselves. They attribute their creations to the subconscious mind, to the dream world. The creations appear more like the result of the unconscious than of the subconscious mind — unconscious of order and humanity and devoid of meaning.

Henri Rousseau, Gauguin, Matisse, Picasso and the surrealist Salvador Dali are master modernists; they have a horde of followers, admirers and imitators.

It is difficult to separate the imposters from the modernists who are sincere. We do know however that the road to hell is paved with good intentions. Sincerity does not mean greatness, and all painting is not art any more than all singing is music. We must recognize, however, that some of the modernists such as Van Gogh and Cézanne have made some important contributions and that the expressionists helped break down art's slavery to organic, realistic values.

George Grosz, who is often classed as a modernist, is essentially an illustrator and caricaturist. His illustration is of the highest order. It is on the brink of great universal art. His composition is not dynamic but his characterization is magnificent. His color is subtle. His line is clumsy, with a kind of clumsiness that lends it-self to social satire. His caustic art may lack universal greatness, but it is a most significant expression of the contemporary social scene. He is a genius in showing how ridiculous man can be.

A modern artist emulating the art of another culture or period is ludicrous to those who are conscious of social forces in art and of historical art progression. Picasso's "classic period" consists of a multitude of gray, brown or muddy colored oversized sketches drawn with a brush. They are obviously childlike copies of classic pieces of sculpture. A bad imitation of classic art or emulation of the African primitives is of no value to civilization or to modern culture.

Those who believe that the individual is above so-ciety, that personal happiness is separate from social welfare, are the major supporters of expressionism. Modernist art reflects the forces that sponsor it.

EXPRESSIONISM AND MOUTHWASH

Many of us ask how it is possible that the disorgan-ized modernist art should achieve such great recogni-tion. Why should a product that has no universal char-acter or social value be acclaimed? What specific forces made expressionism art?

Before we go into consideration of the various social implications, we must recognize that art is a marketable commodity. A multitude of products are dependent more on fashion and trend than on utility. Often fashion and function are completely divorced from each other.

A society leader appears in a new style of dress. An actress informs us that her beautiful complexion is due to smoking a certain brand of cigarettes. A scientist keeps in good health by gargling with a certain brand of mouthwash. A social giant proclaims a new art. Masses of people follow the social leaders in proclaiming the latest trend. We are generally unintelligent consumers.

Picasso's portrait of a man without a head is not much more bizarre than some of the hats that are being worn by women. Wearing open-toed sandals and a fur coat at the same time is not any more incongruous than a painting of the skeleton of a horse hung in a bedroom or salon.

These art atrocities are not as directly devastating to culture as are the acts committed by certain political dictators. Yet the dictators were elected by great masses of people. Propaganda, publicity and intimidation achieved what most intelligent persons believed could not possibly happen — the enemies of social progress were elected.

The ascendancy of an artist is achieved by the same means as the rise of a politician. A barrage of publicity is released, some new or unusual mannerism or rare eccentricity is used as a slogan. Then follows the formation of a cult. At first the cult is exclusive, later it comes into fashion.

Not joining the cult means not being among the elite. A gentleman or a lady who does not wish to feel ostracized must learn to love Picasso and Dali, or at least to pretend to do so. Social ostracism is employed as a weapon in art movements as well as in political movements.

Publicity, the propaganda of merchants, is a powerful force; it breaks down thinking, logic and even common horse sense. We all succumb to it sooner or later. If we do not follow the highly publicized trends and fashions we are made to feel inferior, out of step with the world, old-fashioned. Often we are even branded as eccentric and anti-social if we do not follow the dictates of advertising.

Nearly all of us are potential victims of the comic, the bizarre and the unusual. Circuses are supposedly intended primarily for children, yet adults laugh the loudest at the clown. Multitudes flock to see the freaks. How many people would not stop to look at a man walking on his head?

Modernist art walks on its head. It glorifies individual expression at the expense of society. It expresses the bizarre, it lacks social qualities and human values.

The greater part of expressionism is like a circus, a passing show that amuses but does not stimulate or inspire high human sentiments or actions.

The merchants in art have succeeded in marketing art as an amusement. Art is sold to the public in the same way as vulgar shows, circuses, patent medicines and curealls.

CHAPTER NINE

PRESENT-DAY ART

PRESENT-DAY ART

EXPRESSIONISM went out of favor soon after the economic crash in 1930. However, the modernist groups still survive. The champions of expressionism have not given up their battle to make art purely individualistic and completely abstract. Many artists and lay people sincerely believe in the cause. Some artists justify their shortcomings by pointing to the same shortcomings in an internationally famous painter like Picasso.

Surrealism, futurism, cubism and dadaism are the outstanding schools of expressionism.

Surrealism expresses the subconscious experience of the dream world.

Futurism concentrates on movement, multiple action. The futurist expresses the machine age in a chaotic jumble of varied movements.

The cubist bases his art on a cube or other geometric shape. His expression is also characterized by unorderliness.

Dadaism is a childlike, naive form of personal expression.

We have to remember that all the modernist art expressions revolve around the individual artist, no matter to which group he belongs, whether it is one ism or another. Neither aesthetic law nor social values nor the character of the medium is considered to any serious extent by the modernist.

Expressionism is negative in its universal, social and technical aspects. Only its individual expression is of a positive nature.

As long as extreme individualism survives, expressionist art will no doubt play its part.

RECENT CHANGES IN AMERICAN ART

The greater part of American art has definitely changed in character in the past few years. The current American art movement aims mainly at social subjects and the contemporary scene. It expresses group character and mass movement. Portraits are not in vogue now, paintings of the social scene are predominant.

Artists who have been entirely unrecognized for years have been raised to leadership because they paint the American scene. Abstract form and subjective expression, the chief characteristics of expressionism, have become secondary. The subject has become of vital importance.

Exposition, not expression, is the main characteristic in art today. Illustration has again been raised to a dignified position. Recent paintings express ideas that are neither surrealistic, cubistic or futuristic, nor classic or romantic, but are full of realism and social significance.

The leading American artists of today seek to express social realism, not organic realism or naturalism. They are not interested in painting an organically correct portrait of a man, but are employing the human form as a social symbol. The social scene, not the landscape, is the predominant subject in present-day exhibitions. Artists are again conscious of composition and are becoming aware of the society in which they live.

Benton, Rivera and Orozco are among the outstanding painters of the social scene. They are not escapists, nor are they extreme individualists. They do not sit in their attics and wait for inspiration. They are extremely socially conscious. They study their society and interpret graphically, each in his own manner and style. Though a great number of American artists have not yet succeeded in throwing off their early influences, they are gradually coming under the sway of the American-scene movement.

SOCIAL FORCES AND " THE AMERICAN SCENE "

The depression was mainly responsible for " The American-Scene " movement. Before our economic collapse artists migrated to Europe to escape the American scene. The depression and the resultant fall of the dollar brought the artists back and forced them to paint their native environment.

We have ceased to admire all of French art and we have become very proud of our own, though only a few years ago, we neglected or despised it. The depression forced us to become conscious of our own society and of our own art.

Franklin D. Roosevelt can be considered the virtual leader of the new school of American art. He swayed public opinion in art just as much as in commerce and industry. He took the artist out of his attic and put him into a modern shop.

When Roosevelt set out to employ professional and nonprofessional workers in public works projects, he included the artist among them. The artist was taken out of his idealist haven and was put right next to the engineer, the farmer and the bricklayer. He began to consider himself a worker instead of an inspired spirit. He even formed a union.

The democratic party of ancient Athens, under the leadership of Pericles, really created the first "new deal." The rule of Pericles brought about a complete change in the social character of the Athenian state. Not only did Pericles undertake to make every citizen conscious of his society but, through a great building and cultural program, he inspired art-consciousness. Like Roosevelt, Pericles belonged to an aristocratic family. He sought the advice of scholars and philosophers just as Roosevelt sought the advice of sociologists and economists.

In spite of his achievement, Pericles had a great number of enemies. Dramatists and satirists were encouraged and employed by the opposition to ridicule and vilify him. Yet without exception historians through the ages have shown great admiration for the ancient Athenian state. Our schoolbooks are full of the glory of the Periclean age. Many people admire neo-classic art, which is an imitation of Greek art of the period of Pericles.

The enemies of the democratic party did not praise the great art and building projects of Athens. They accused Pericles of squandering the people's money. Yet the period of his rule gave birth to philosophers, dramatists, architects, sculptors, painters and poets whose works have survived to this day.

Nowadays we have remarkable machines that can produce thousands of times as much goods as any number of slaves. Our citizens have even more time for social interests and cultural activities than did the ancient Greeks. Because of the leisure created by the machine modern society can produce even greater art and science characteristic of our industrial civilization, just as Athenian democracy produced great artists and philosophers characteristic of a craft civilization.

Contemporary art in America expresses the spirit of the American people just as classic art expressed the spirit of ancient Athens. " The American Scene," one of the legitimate children of the New Deal, is the living slogan in American art today.

The newly formed art projects were informed that the administration would accept and pay only for art of the American scene. The art brought back from France, Spain or any other European country would not be accepted. That is when " The American Scene " in art was legally born.

THE SOCIAL THEME IN THE ARTS

Today social consciousness manifests itself in every one of the arts. The cinema, drama and literature have changed greatly. New dramatists and novelists have arisen, depicting the American scene.

Slapstick comedies have disappeared. Sex dramas have declined. Mystery plays are not much heard of. The melodrama is outmoded. Displays of nudity are box office failures. Vaudeville has virtually vanished.

Many successful theatrical performances are social in character. *It Can't Happen Here, Knickerbocker Holiday, Of Mice and Men, Pins and Needles, Awake and Sing, Julius Caesar* (in modern version) and *Tobacco Road* are only a few of the numerous social plays that have been produced in recent years.

The moving pictures have had their share of social themes. Some, if not most, of the biggest box office successes have been pictures with social content. In spite of the fact that the moving picture theater is frequently used by the public as a means of escape and relaxation, the social picture is strongly acclaimed.

Hollywood will not and cannot swing entirely to the production of social pictures for a number of reasons. But it is important to recognize that for the past few years social movies have been box office successes.

John Steinbeck, James Farrell, Ernest Hemingway, Richard Wright and Sinclair Lewis are only a few of the fiction writers who have been depicting the American scene.

A great number of nonfiction books dealing with the social scene have been published. Of these Lewis Mumford's *Technics and Civilization* and *The Culture of Cities* are probably the most important.

Poets, too, are dealing with the social scene. Dancers have been popularizing social dances. Some popular songs are social in content. The spirit of the social scene is still growing in all the arts.

ART APPRECIATION AND THE DEPRESSION

A revolutionary change has taken place in American life since the economic crash. Since the year 1930 the majority of American people have become more socially conscious. They have expressed this social consciousness by beginning to take a more active interest in the society in which they live. The basic social force, namely economics, brought about the awakening. The same force helped revive their creative instincts.

With the awakening of social consciousness the American citizen began to discard many phases of the outworn and outmoded emotional forms of expression. He looked about him in search of new emotional outlets.

Great numbers of men and women were suddenly burdened with added leisure hours at the same time that their financial status had sunk. The new leisure gave them time to search for new emotional and mental outlets and the financial difficulties forced them to seek free recreation. They discovered the museum, the art gallery, the concert hall and the free symphony.

Never in the history of America have such tremendous throngs attended concerts and art exhibitions as in the past few years. The free WPA concerts have been acclaimed by millions of people. Lectures on art and museum tours have been attended by multitudes.

Many have taken to studying art mediums. Thousands are attending art classes. Great numbers of men and women are studying music and joining choruses. Many have found an interest in forums, literary groups and current topic discussions.

Art in all mediums has become a greater social force.

Art is enriching the lives of our citizens. We may even soon come to the realization that organized form is not the monopoly of art, that composition or organization is also the basis for society.

THE EASEL PAINTING AND THE MURAL

During the Renaissance, Florence and Rome, cities of cathedrals, produced the outstanding murals. Venice, the city of wealthy homes, produced the outstanding easel paintings.

The mural is playing a major role in the social construction of the new Mexican state. The Mexican government is sponsoring mural art to as large an extent as Renaissance Florence and Rome did. The reasons for the supremacy of the mural in Mexican art are the same as the reasons for its supremacy in fifteenth- and sixteenth-century Florence and Rome.

Pictures are attached to walls. The dimension of the wall and the character of the building are the deciding factors in the kind of art to be employed.

The walls of a home require small oils, water colors or drawings. The walls of a public building are large and spacious and therefore require mural art. Thus murals are characteristic of a society that constructs public buildings.

Another major reason for the mural is that it is an effective means for educating illiterate people. It lends itself better to the social theme than does the small painting. The Mexican government is teaching the ideals of social construction to its primitive, illiterate, feudal masses by means of the mural, just as the Catholic Church taught the people its concepts by means of mural art.

In the United States the mural was not popular until the Roosevelt administration began its building program. Murals are now extensively employed in federal public buildings. Easel paintings are, however, still more numerous than murals.

Small paintings are not being purchased to any considerable degree at the present time for the simple reason that the upper middle classes, formerly the greatest purchasers of contemporary art, have lost their financial means.

Murals have been used in buildings for private enterprise since the new trend has been started by the government, but not in such large numbers as to give mural art any great importance.

Our building program is not sufficiently great to give much encouragement to mural art. Most artists cling to the easel picture. The public is still partial to the small paintings to which it is accustomed.

The easel painting will probably predominate for some time to come, but the mural will undoubtedly grow in popularity. When the American mural does reach supremacy it will surely be a dynamic art, unlike the static forms of the Mexican murals, which are characteristic of a socially backward and slow-moving country.

AMERICAN AND EUROPEAN ART

Present-day American art is completely democratic in spirit. Every artist who paints the American scene expresses himself as he feels impelled to. No one interferes with his personal expression.

Michelangelo was asked to paint the Testament. Titian was commissioned to paint nudes. The American artist is encouraged to paint the American scene. Adherence to the subject is the only restriction, even when the government is the purchaser or sponsor.

The interpretation of the American scene is not dictated. Each artist interprets America according to his own convictions. Some artists glorify the American scene and flatter the *status quo,* while others vilify and satirize it. Because the American artist, like all other creators in this country, is free to express himself as he desires American art exhibitions show the greatest variety of individual expression.

The situation is not at all the same in Europe. Individual expression does not exist in contemporary German art, nor in anything else in the Germany of today. One would expect the Nazi concept of German superiority to foster the creation of a new art. But like all dictators in history Hitler is the champion of pseudo-classic art. His new palace is furnished throughout in the neo-classic style.

The Italian fascist government is spending a vast fortune on excavating the glories of ancient Rome. Very little is spent on contemporary art. What art is now being created in Italy is pseudo-classic. The literature of Italy, as of Germany, is pseudo-classic, or just straight propaganda, without the pretense of art. The drama is of the same ilk.

France and England have been occupied more with self-preservation than with sponsoring art. About Russian art we know very little. The small European countries have not been producing great works of art. However, the Scandinavians have in recent years developed industrial design and creative craft of superb quality.

CLASSICISM AND MODERN CULTURE

Greek art was great and significant because it was true to Greek life. Classicism in our time is a farce because it does not reflect our mode of living. It is not only superficial, but is often employed as an opiate and as an enemy of social welfare. It is used to glorify false ideals and is championed by those who desire to turn society backwards.

There are painters and sculptors in America who

paint and model Greek gods. We do not believe in the Greek gods as did the ancient Greeks. We do not look like Greeks, we do not live like Greeks, yet we have artists who attempt to create like Greeks.

Our culture will not be a true, significant culture so long as we continue building Gothic universities and Greek museums. Gothic architecture was significant in its day. In our modern age of steel it is a symbol of the past. It has no living relationship to modern life.

The finest industrial arts collection in America is housed in a building of ancient Greek design. There is absolutely no relationship between the structure and the objects displayed in it.

Classic architecture was a remarkable expression of a great society. It also expressed the qualities inherent in marble or stone, but it expresses nothing of our industrial age and has no kinship to modern industrial products.

Not only is there a lack of social kinship between ancient Greek architecture and modern concepts and products, but the modern imitation lacks the character and beauty of the original. Ancient Greek buildings were constructed of rich marble and were beautifully colored. The cement or sandstone imitation is dead, gray, inaccurate, and appears ridiculous in a modern setting.

All our arts should be the expression of our age as

Greek art was the expression of its own culture and Egyptian art the expression of its civilization. Ancient Greece would not have been great had she copied the culture of Egypt.

CHAPTER TEN

ART IN EDUCATION

ART IN EDUCATION

THE TRADITIONAL idea of school art is often not only a waste of time but a definite hindrance to the normal growth of the child.

The child's earliest experiences are lasting; they build the child's character. The traditional classroom procedure of having the child draw cubes and cones may have taught him to use the pencil, to learn the medium, and to see direction of line and intensity of light and shade. The weakness in this method of art education lies in the fact that school is a preparation for adult life and that life does not consist of cubes and cones.

The more modern method of having the children draw flowers is no great improvement, for the reason that life does not consist of pretty flowers. However, drawing flowers does encourage spontaneity, because flowers are colorful and if they are real they have some life in them.

Neither the flowers nor the geometric blocks give the growing child the opportunity to express himself. The child's creative mind, his urge to express his feelings, his desire to interpret his new experiences, are not stimulated in the cube or flower classroom.

Child education is not meant to be technique development. Child training is training for life, training the child to meet new experiences intelligently and to learn to act in accordance with his experiences.

The most constructive principle of child education is the creative principle. It is based on recognition of the child's world, his spiritual and psychic life. The creative method gives the child an opportunity and formulates the habit to see, to feel, to interpret, to organize and to create.

Art is one of the most important divisions in the child's education — a division, because art should not be a subject apart, but should be integrated with all the other subjects. Integrated means to be interwoven, combined with every other subject, and not treated as an illustrative medium or as a supplement.

As soon as we recognize that creative art teaches the child to see, to feel, to interpret, to organize and to create, we begin to understand the role of art in child education. If the child is led and trained to create, he is more likely to become a creator in his adult life. Seeing, feeling, interpreting, organizing and creating constitute intelligent living. The right kind of art education helps prepare the child for that kind of living.

A remarkable example of a child's expression is a picture drawn by a pupil in the fourth grade. The boy asked the teacher whether he could draw a picture of heaven. The teacher approved the subject. The boy composed a picture which showed: to the left, a cottage with a sign, " Ice Cream Free "; to the right, another cottage with a sign, " Candy Free "; below, two ponies with a sign, " Free Rides "; in the sky, two angels with shopping bags, an angel with an ice cream cone, another one with a bar of candy; at the very bottom were two big clouds, in each a sign reading, " No Taxes."

That boy comes from a poor home. The father is often unemployed. The family owns a little cottage. The parents had been terribly worried about the taxes and had been discussing their predicament. They saved pennies that might ordinarily have gone to the boy for candy and ice cream to help pay the taxes.

This boy's painting illustrates the child's capacity for imagination, correlation, organization, interpretation and deep feeling. It shows how children are affected by their environment.

Many people treat children as if they were adults and judge them by adult standards. But children live in an imaginary world, they do not see the realities we do. They do not have our outlook or our experience and therefore cannot be expected to create like adults.

The most important urge in a child is toward individual expression. We should guide the child to perceive and conceive aesthetic principles. We should point out the elements of variety and movement. We must emphasize the importance of harmony and unity. But all of these must be brought out simply in relation to the specific problem. We cannot use a social approach in teaching art to a child because society has no meaning to the child. Children should be taught to compose images of their own world, a world of limited experience and unlimited imagination.

The teacher should never insist on a realistic interpretation of the subject. The realism of the subject may be extremely important to the adult but has no significance to the child, who has not assimilated enough of reality to be able to evaluate it. The subject or object is a vague symbol to the child, not a reality.

The child should be encouraged to create a variety of abstract, imaginary forms in rhythmic movement, in pure, glowing colors, harmonized and unified into one picture. The child comprehends easily the universal principles of composition, variety becomes meaningful to him at an early stage, and movement is very intriguing to him. Harmony and unity take on meaning as the child grows older. Understanding of organization can be developed in the child through the proper art education.

ART AS PROPAGANDA AND EDUCATION

Art is often anti-social propaganda. It has been used not only as an escapist drug but for impressing false ideas on the public mind.

Why do commercial firms use posters as one of the principal means of advertising their products? Because certain combinations of colors and forms attract attention and become imprinted on the mind. Many commercial posters exaggerate and some actually misrepresent.

Music lifts our spirits and inspires us to do great deeds. Music has also been used to inspire hatred and slaughter. A band with its martial music is responsible for many a battle cry.

The drama has been used to express the human spirit, to inspire, teach and entertain audiences. It has also been used for vicious propaganda, as a means of distorting and misrepresenting the truth.

Through the ages art mediums have been employed for anti-social propaganda. We must, however, differentiate between what is often considered to be destructive propaganda and what actually is destructive propaganda. Not all propaganda has a harmful effect on society.

" Propaganda " means transmittance of an idea. We should therefore decide whether the idea is good or bad, constructive or destructive. If the propaganda is socially constructive it is educational in value.

Education is often called propaganda because it propagates new ideas. The new concepts are often contrary to the established opinion. However, the fact that the new concepts have no precedent does not mean that they are not beneficial.

A major difference between propaganda and education is that propaganda states only one side of a case, while education seeks to bring out all sides. The propagandist insists that his authority be accepted without question. The educator presents all sides from which he wants the conclusions to be derived.

We must keep in mind the fact that political powers often do not differentiate between propaganda and education. Under a dictatorship, education, like art, becomes propaganda, for the simple reason that a dictatorship cannot and will not permit both sides of a problem to be considered and discussed. True education can exist only in a democracy.

We must, therefore, conclude that education can be considered propaganda because it propagates ideas. But propaganda is never education if it presents only one side and does not involve the function of thinking.

Every great artist can be called a propagandist because he expresses a dominant idea or feeling and because his concept is concentrated and emphatic, and appeals to the emotions as well as to the mind. Aristophanes, Dante, Michelangelo, Rembrandt, Shakespeare and Beethoven were great propagandists.

The escape into art has not been as successful as some believe. The art that really affects us does not impel us to escape. On the contrary, great art fosters social consciousness through the associative process.

When we look at an Egyptian work of art we immediately visualize Egyptian civilization. When we look at an ancient Greek work of art we visualize the beauty and greatness of ancient Greek society. A painting by Titian makes us think of the kind of life the Venetians of the Renaissance led.

We cannot escape being affected and influenced by the dynamic power and movement of the titanic murals of Michelangelo. Not only do we visualize by association the society in which his art was created, but we are affected by the harmony of action and by the unity of organization. Harmony and unity are also everyday problems and social objectives.

Art composition can make us conscious of the organization in our social life. The degree of such consciousness depends on the ability to associate compositional values in art with the organizational aspects of social living.

When the artist aspires toward a more joyous life and inspires society toward progress through an art medium, he is a propagandist. Great artists always sought greater aesthetic truth and expression and greater social freedom. They were, therefore, ideal propagandists. The master artists of history not only were influenced by social forces, but also created social forces by expressing great, aesthetic, universal ideals.

Many people will accept new concepts in the arts more readily than they will new economic or political ideas, because the latter may endanger personal economic security or supremacy. It is, therefore, true that new social values often reach the public through art before they affect us through economic means or political sources.

THE ARTIST AS TEACHER

Objective criticism stimulates subjective expression. A successful teacher is one who can be objective in his approach to the student's work. A successful artist is usually subjective. One who can be subjective in his art and objective in his teaching can be both a successful artist and a successful teacher.

A great artist-teacher of my acquaintance painted very spontaneously in a neutral key, in a distinctly chosen and limited palette. Yet many of his students painted tightly, some in low key, others in high, some in a heavy technique, others in transparent pigment; some used small brushes, some large ones, others employed the palette knife. This artist-teacher had a psychological approach. He studied the pupil's character and encouraged the choice of the technique which best suited the student's temperament.

Many creative artists are poor teachers because they are just as subjective about the expression of others as they are about their own. They are essentially undemocratic because they deny others the right of personal expression. They justify their own individual expression on the ground of genius and not on the basis of creative freedom.

A teacher who encourages or permits his students to emulate his personal characteristics, mannerisms, style or technique is not inspiring the creation of true art. The young artist must be taught to be creative and original from the beginning of his training, if he is to produce significant work early in his art career. It takes many years to discard a teacher's superimposed style and technique before becoming free to express oneself naturally. Often genuine personal expression is forever killed in the regimented classroom.

The art teacher must have a sympathetic understanding of the character of each pupil and a thorough knowledge of the technical problems involved. Moreover, he must comprehend and feel the spiritual and emotional aspects of art by doing creative work himself.

LEARNING TO DRAW

Every person who can learn to write can learn to draw and paint. What the average layman believes is his inability to draw is really his inability to see. When there is a form running from left to right and he draws it from right to left, it is because he cannot see correctly. When a beginning art student draws the head of the model one-fifth the size of the body instead of one-eighth or one-seventh, it is because his untrained eye cannot see proportion, not because he cannot draw.

A great artist puts distinct character into his drawing and painting. We call that character his style. Distinctive style and the expression of significant concepts cannot be taught. No teacher can make a creative artist out of someone who simply does not have the capacity to create. A good teacher can, however, make a painter or a sculptor out of any intelligent person.

The process of learning to draw is basically not different from the process of learning to write. First you learn to observe, then to put down forms in their correct proportions. Then you learn to organize a variety of forms. Composing a picture is essentially not different from composing a sentence, paragraph or chapter. An art composition can be made simple or complex, as a literary unit can consist of one sentence or of many chapters.

An understanding of perspective and of the laws governing light and shade is a great aid in learning to see form. The knowledge of anatomy is a great help in drawing the figure. Knowing that a line should go in a certain direction helps one to see the direction of the line. We recognize a shade value if we know that it should be there. Knowing that a muscle is situated in a specific place helps us to find it.

We are psychologically so constituted that perception depends on association. It is not, however, absolutely necessary to have a knowledge of perspective and *chiaroscuro* (light and shade) in order to draw forms, nor is it imperative to know anatomy in order to draw the figure.

Associations do not necessarily have to be made by way of optical laws or anatomic charts. Within the process of evaluating and measuring proportions association takes place. Comparison of the size of the head with that of the arm, of the length of the arm with that of the leg, is a process of association. Thus we learn to draw by acquiring the habit of associating one part of the figure or object with the other part or parts.

ART IN ADULT EDUCATION

The traditional notion of education, meaning education for those between the ages of seven and seventeen, has gone the way of the horse and buggy. Education no longer means reading, writing and arithmetic. Nor does it mean the study of higher mathematics, of the sciences and philosophy, of history and the classics. Familiarity with these no doubt is a part of culture, but it does not make a person educated. These accomplishments by no means constitute a modern education.

With the coming of more leisure time there was born a need for a new kind of education, a need for leisure time cultural activities. The sixteen hours of each day which we spend in active living can be spent constructively or destructively, in a cultural manner or in a vulgar fashion. Six or eight hours of the sixteen are spent in working to gain a livelihood. How are we going to spend the remaining eight or ten hours?

The ancient Athenians had slaves who did most of their work, as our machines do most of our work. They had much leisure time in which they studied social problems, attended the theater, participated in discussions and enjoyed the fine arts. They built a great civilization and created a magnificent culture which expressed the characteristics of their craft society.

Are we going to build a great civilization on the basis of our industrial society, or are we going to use our leisure time in a subversive, destructive manner? Either is possible. There is no intermediate road. Life means action and action is either constructive or destructive. Which is our life, which is our action going to be?

The child is no longer the only member of society

that has to be educated. The progress of the machine was much too fast for the habit-ridden parent and the tradition-bound adult. The machine has quite suddenly brought to the adult much more leisure time than he ever had before. But that is a blessing which can easily be turned into a curse. Is the adult going to turn this leisure time into creative, constructive channels or into demoralizing decadence?

Are parents going to keep up with their children, or are they going to stagnate and thus hamper the progress of their sons and daughters? Do parents want their children to feel that they are backward? The answer is, " No." Do most people want to be bored, vulgar, ignorant, destructive? The answer is, " No." Then we must have adult education.

Adult education differs in method and procedure from traditional child education. The average adult cherishes a set of pre-established conceptions and ideas which do not fit into an industrial society, while the child has an open, fresh mind. We can easily compare the child's mind to an empty box, the adult's to a filled box. Only one process is necessary in order to fill the empty box with the proper articles; but with the box that has already been filled with the wrong ingredients, the task is a dual one. First we must empty the box of the wrong ingredients, then replace them with the right matter.

Information given to a child is rarely a contradiction

to a conception already established, whereas to the adult who has been educated in craft concepts new information nearly always is a contradiction. We are slaves of habit. To teach typing to a person who has never studied it is much easier than to teach the right method of typing to one who has been using a wrong method for years.

Furthermore, adult education deals with individuals who are much more unlike one another than are children. Sixth grade children may generally be divided into two classes, the less intelligent and the more intelligent. Among twenty adults in a class you may find no two alike because of the vast difference in education and background.

One thing that nearly all adults have in common with children is that they are gregarious and enjoy group action. Adult education must, therefore, be a social activity rather than a formal, restricted classroom procedure. Adults cannot be forced to come to class.

Educators are well aware of the fact that illiteracy still haunts our national culture. There is a nation-wide movement to eradicate this undemocratic, un-American aspect of our society. A literacy program is one of the major divisions of nearly all adult education programs and public evening schools.

The advantages of being an American citizen have

become quite obvious of late. Individuals who have for many years been concerned only with their jobs have become conscious of their social life and their obligations and responsibilities to their government.

Educators realize that the citizenship certificate does not make true citizens. It grants the right of citizenship, but not the consciousness. True democratic citizenship must be functional. The making of a functioning citizen requires more than literacy and a birth or citizenship certificate. A functioning citizen is an acting citizen, a participant in the activities of his society, culturally and politically.

The democratic citizen must function constructively and socially in his daily life. He must have activities which give him the opportunity to express himself emotionally and intellectually as well as physically.

The fine arts are the most stimulating cultural activities. The art mediums are of interest to nearly all individuals either as an activity or as an appreciation. For that reason the arts are an important division of adult education.

Educators know that cultural activities in leisure time are a means for preserving democracy. Leisure time without constructive activities is a potential force for the elimination of democracy. Economic security is basic but cultural activity is essential in a democratic country.

Leaders in adult education recognize that all the citizens must have activities within their scope and sphere and that all people must be provided with leadership and guidance.

A great number of persons still look upon art as a subject to appreciate but not one in which to participate. In order to get a multitude of people to draw, paint, carve, etc., we must get out of the layman's mind the erroneous idea that he must have a special talent.

It should be emphasized that in order to appreciate an art fully we must practice it ourselves. By painting a little we begin to appreciate the real significance of painting. The adult should be encouraged to express in his art his feelings and concepts.

Adult education should — and in time will — consist mainly of cultural activities because they are creative and entertaining; they can be enjoyed by active participation or by enjoyable reception. Drawing, painting, carving, playing a musical instrument are instinctive with man. As soon as the inhibitions are removed the instinct reveals itself.

That pleasure is derived from looking at art and listening to music is undeniable. People should be guided into greater appreciation. They must be taught to recognize all the aspects of art and thus enrich their lives.

Compositional principles are transferable from art to other fields. The practice of harmony and unity in art can by association be transferred into other social, everyday activities.

CURRENT AND LIVE MATERIALS IN ADULT EDUCATION

Education has for years been looked upon as an unpleasant necessity and a painful process. Learning is traditionally associated with Gothic colleges and classic libraries. Those who look backward, who turn to the ancients and have no inclination to look forward, are considered cultured persons. Symbols of the past are the only materials employed in many classrooms.

Our grandfathers believed that education and play are unrelated, that they are opposites. Education has always been considered constructive, while play was looked upon by many practical persons as a waste of time and energy. Some educational systems still operate on the theory that education is divorced from play. However, educational organizations are accepting the concept that play and education are related.

Modern teachers are discarding the traditional, outworn ideas and notions. We know that learning can be a joy to the adult as well as to the child. We recognize that there is a natural desire for leisure and must realize that an industrial society can provide the coveted leisure. We should encourage every individual to express himself, to do, to create. The creative aspect of craft is entirely lacking in industrial work. The worker in a modern factory has no opportunity to express himself as did the ancient craftsman. However, the modern industrial worker has a far greater number of leisure hours than the craftsman had.

The problem is how the adult should express himself. Should our citizens spend their leisure hours in a democratic way or should they follow the example of some European countries? It is up to the leaders and teachers. Educators of adults face a great and serious problem in this changing world. It is not an easy matter to lead people from the habitual craft habits into thought processes and actions which are functional and in keeping with industrial progress and tempo.

We cannot dig up ancient skeletons of learning and feed them to adults. We must provide fresh, invigorating mental food, in keeping with the needs of modern industrial life. Few are interested in learning of the greatness of past civilizations. Many are interested in their surroundings, in everyday occurrences. By means of the everyday activities adults become aware of new concepts and conscious of the problems that grow out of industrial progress.

Current and live materials are invigorating, fresh and inspiring. They affect our lives, and what affects our lives interests us. Education is found not only in a library or a formalized schoolroom, but also in daily life. The education of life is the primary concern of every adult and is therefore the most effective kind of adult education. Adult classes, whether in sociology, literature or art, should deal with live materials.

Strict departmentalism is another relic of the past. Life is not divided into distinct departments. Education therefore should not be divided into separate departments. If anything is a part of our life, it should be a part of our education.

A flight around the world in record time is current and live material. It is constructive material for a discussion class, for a writing and language class, for a drawing and painting class, for a sculpture class. Some would talk about the history-making flight, others would write about it, some would draw or paint it, others would carve or model it. Each would express himself in his medium, in his favorite style and manner. This is democracy, this is adult education. This is using current and live materials.

A ball game is live and current material for an adult education class. There seem to be varied opinions on ball playing. Some consider ball games a recreation, others look upon them as exercise, and there are those who think they are a form of gambling. A ball game can be discussed, written about, drawn or painted. Sport can enrich the mind and the spirit as well as the body.

To the ancient Greeks sports were not purely physical, mere muscle developers. We know more about human nature, about psychology, than the classic Greeks did. We know how to co-ordinate the mind and the body. But we are departmentalized, we specialize. Some prefer to have a strong body with a weak head, others a strong head on a weak body. We have not yet learned to co-ordinate our lives.

Farmers, factory workers and miners are extremely interesting study material. Coal mining can start a discussion or a reading and writing lesson; drawings can be made of the miners. A Belgian artist, Meunier, made his reputation with painting and modeling coal miners. Miners are current and live material.

Our everyday life is full of a great variety of rhythmic movement which can be harmonized and unified. The rhythmic movements can be interpreted and expressed in discussion, in writing, in drawing and painting, in sculpture and in music. The rhythm of life is significant material for adult education.

SPECIFIC OBJECTIVES OF AN ADULT EDUCATION ART PROGRAM

An adult education art program should not aim to train artists. Its objectives should be:

1. To introduce the public to the relationship between art composition and social organization.

2. To teach the integration of art principles in everyday life.

3. To provide for the adult a cultural and constructive leisure time activity.

4. To emphasize the relationship between art and industry.

SPECIFIC METHODS TO BE EMPLOYED IN AN
ADULT EDUCATION ART PROGRAM

I. Employment of educationally sound methods in dealing with adults:

1. Teaching creative art by objective criticism, the teacher always keeping in mind that objective criticism stimulates subjective expression.

2. Giving the student what he wants until the teacher can influence him to want what he needs.

3. Encouraging the student to correlate his daily experience with the activities of the class.

4. Conducting the class or group work in an informal manner.

II. Teaching of art structure and composition by analogy with social structure and composition. This can best be done by emphasizing the relationship of:

1. Variety in art and in life.

2. Harmony in art and in social life.

3. Action in art and in social progress.

4. Unity in art and in society.

III. Teaching of art history and contemporary art analysis from four approaches:

1. The *aesthetic,* which is of universal significance.
2. The *social,* which brings out the character of the society in which the art is created.
3. The *individual,* which emphasizes the personal expression of the artist.
4. The *technical,* which deals with the aspects of the medium and technique.

WHERE ART IS LEADING

Contemporary thought on art is in a transitional stage. While Europe has not been very conscious of its art in recent years, American art-consciousness has greatly increased. Most art critics have turned to the social scene. Philosophers today recognize art as a significant social force. Some of the exponents of expressionism are still being read but their influence is declining rapidly.

Thomas Craven has brought art down from its ivory tower. Hendrik Van Loon has humanized art history. Lewis Mumford more than anyone else has succeeded in presenting art in its relationship to science, economics and all the aspects of progressing civilization. The social aspect of art is undoubtedly coming to the top.

However, numerous schools, colleges and universities still preach neo-classicism; a few insist on realism. Several institutions of higher learning have only a few years ago accepted modernism. Art is still kept apart as an entity by itself, unrelated to other fields of human endeavor. Art is still commonly thought of as unscientific, and science as inartistic.

Those institutions, however, that are keeping up with industrial progress have combined art and science courses and are training industrial designers who will no doubt be the leaders of the aesthetics of the future. The industrial designer reaches the people in home and street, in parlor and kitchen, on highway, railway and sidewalk. He speaks a language all can understand, the language of function, utility as well as of beauty.

Industrial designing is undoubtedly one of the greatest revolutionary forces in our society. This force more than any political movement tends to make life significant aesthetically as well as physically. No political reaction or decadence can stop this onrushing, dynamic union between art and science.

Composition has been considered important by all schools of art with the exception of expressionism. However, the traditional schools did not recognize composition as the basic element of beauty. Compositional values were understood not as human values, but as purely technical aspects. Thus art was separated from life, art principles were estranged from social values.

We are now beginning to integrate all life activities. We are not yet conscious of the co-ordinating force of art and science and its combined integration with life, but we are definitely on the road to organizing all human expression.

As we must live with love in order to appreciate love, so must we live with art in order to appreciate art. Art can be significant only if it is part of our lives, if it is interwoven with all our being and if it is an integral part of our character.

In order to live with art, in order to lead an aesthetic life, the individual must have freedom to express himself in his leisure time. He must become aware of the significance of harmony and unity and conscious of the enormous variety and dynamic movement of his society. He must recognize that living with art means living with orderliness.

The individual must come to the realization that art is reaching us through the machine and industry. It is becoming a factor in our clothes and home furnishings, in our parlors and kitchens, in spite of reactionary attempts to retain the craft notion that art belongs in the salon, gallery and museum.

Painting, music, literature and drama are becoming social and are demonstrating that composition can be achieved in the spirit of creation and for the benefit of society. Soon everything will have to be planned and organized. The town and city will in the near future be designed and composed like a work of art.

Artists are human! Their works are the products of social experience. The emotion expressed in them as well as the logic of their organization and the character of their content must be communicable. If art is to be communicable, it must be created in compositional values; and if art is to be completely appreciated, society must become conscious of the significance of organization and composition.

Social organization and individual expression combined will lead our civilization onward. One without the other is sterile. In art also, individual expression must be in harmony with organizational and compositional principles. Man is both individual and social, and such must his art be.

SUGGESTED READING

IF THIS BOOK has fulfilled its purpose, it has not only given the reader a basic understanding of the significance of art, but has also inspired a desire for a more extensive study of the subject.

The Arts, by Hendrik van Loon. A colorfully written history of the arts, with illustrations by the author.

Art in the Western World, by David M. Robb and J. J. Garrison. An account of the expression and value of art in Western civilization. The book discusses the major works of the outstanding artists and the materials and techniques. About 400 illustrations.

An Illustrated Handbook of Art History, by Frank J. Roos, Jr. Contains over two thousand illustrations which cover Western art from the prehistoric period to the present. A complete history of art in pictures.

The Life of Greece, by Will Durant. A vivid picture of the golden age of Greece with an interesting comparison of the life of Greece with our life of today.

The Civilization of the Renaissance, by Jacob Burckhardt. The book is a complete pageant of Renaissance Italy. 421 reproductions.

Men of Art, by Thomas Craven. An illuminating and comprehensive study of outstanding artists from Giotto to the present day.

Art in America, edited by Holger Cahill and Alfred H. Barr, Jr., with over 300 illustrations, 17 in full color. The book shows the development of American art in all its forms: painting, sculpture, architecture, industrial arts, mural painting, photography, theatre arts and the motion picture.

Modern Art, by Thomas Craven. An analysis of modern art movements. A discussion of the meaning of modern art and a vivid presentation of the lives of the outstanding modernist artists.

Primer of Modern Art, by C. Cheney. An outline of the various movements in the arts. A complete presentation of the outstanding expressionists and their followers.

Understanding the Arts, by Helen Gardner. The book embraces architecture, painting and sculpture and the minor arts from the earliest times to the present day. The author analyzes the aesthetic and technical aspects of all mediums.

Art as Experience, by John Dewey. America's outstanding philosopher discusses the place of art in the life of man.

Art Principles in Practice, by Henry R. Poore. The book deals with principles of art which are interesting and stimulating to the art student.

Art and Society, by Herbert Read. The author surveys the world's art not as an isolated activity but as one related to the culture and societies from which it flowers. He begins with prehistoric art and ends the book with an analysis of art in our day.

Technics and Civilization, by Lewis Mumford. A remarkable analysis of technology and its relationship to art and life from early times to the present day. The author traces the growth of the machine and its influence on humanity and its culture.

The Culture of Cities, by Lewis Mumford. The new role of Cities and Regions in modern civilization. The author tells how the cities have grown from simple towns of the medieval period to the huge complex roaring cities of the twentieth century. Mr. Mumford gives the factors that have conditioned the size, growth and cultural character of cities. He also discusses the possibilities for creating form and order in our present civilization.

Architecture and Modern Life, by Baker Brownell and Frank Lloyd Wright. An eminent architect and a student of contemporary thought survey the field of architecture in its relation to our modern social structure, define present trends, and dare to prophesy a future when society and architecture will complement each other in expressing the ideals of a new and vital civilization.

Design This Day: The Technique of Order in the Machine Age, by Walter Dorwin Teague. A magnificent analysis of the principles and purposes of design in modern life explaining the function and revolutionary influence of design in the world of today. 128 pages of illustrations.

Art and the Machine, by Sheldon and Martha Cheney. An account of industrial design in 20th-Century America. Illustrated.

Horizons, by N. B. Geddes. An outline of the future of design in industry and in everyday life. Illustrated.

The Art Spirit, by Robert Henri. Notes, articles, fragments of letters and talks to students on the conception and technique of the art of painting.

Gist of Art, by John Sloan. An outstanding American artist discusses techniques and materials, principles and practices in the classroom and studio. Illustrated.

Pictorial Composition: The Critical Judgment of Pictures, by Henry R. Poore. This book, published thirty-six years ago, sets forth an analysis of pictorial processes which, while of special interest to the artist and photographer, is intended also to aid the layman in his appreciation of pictorial arrangement.

Color in Everyday Life, by Louis Weinberg. A manual for lay students, artisans and artists on the principles of color combination and color arrangement, and their applications in dress, home, business, the theatre and community play.

The New Art Education, by R. M. Pearson. A definite presentation of modern methods employed to get students to release and express their own distinctive artistic talents. Illustrated.

The Integrated School Art Program, by Leon L. Winslow. A sound and practical presentation of art education methods and principles emphasizing the integration of art programs with all phases of school and daily life activity. Illustrated.

COLOPHON

This book is composed on the Linotype in Baskerville, a modern adaption of the type designed by John Baskerville (1706–1775) at Birmingham, England, for his own private press. His letters, with contrasting light and heavy strokes, were considered delicate and refined by many of his contemporaries who were more appreciative of the then-prevalent rugged and massive English fonts. Nevertheless, his punches and matrices definitely influenced later European type-design, particularly in France and Italy. Many typographers concede his original face to be the forerunner of the " modern " group of type-faces.

Typography, printing, and binding by the Plimpton Press, Norwood, Massachusetts — LaPorte, Indiana.

Text paper (Novel Antique) by the S. D. Warren Company. Cloth (Bancroft Buckram) by Albert D. Smith & Company.

A. KROCH AND SON · PUBLISHERS